THE BOOK OF EDEN

Genesis 2-3

"... where we think again about the Bible on women and men and we start with a correct understanding of what happened in the Garden of Eden back in the beginning."

BRUCE C. E. FLEMING

Founder of the Tru316 Project (Tru316.com)

Based on the work of Joy Fleming. PhD, PsyD

with study guides by

Joanne Guarnieri Hagemeyer

"While most readers will be familiar with John 3:16, the Flemings throw open a window of fresh air on another vital "3:16" text. In a captivating style that blends diligent study of several relevant biblical passages with gutsy personal stories, this couple has torn down barriers that restrict women in the church, family and workplace. Be prepared to revisit your assumptions! Personally, my reading of this book has reassured me that women are equal in the kingdom."

—Dr. Daryl F. Busby
Former Dean of Canadian Baptist Seminary in Langley BC

"I'm profoundly grateful for the Flemings' work--indeed, their lifetime of work--which shines a clarifying light on some of the most profound and troublesome passages in Genesis: Are women cursed by God? Did God punish Eve and all women by increasing pain in childbirth? Did God sanction the ruling of men over women? Centuries of disvalue on women and a distortion of God's design for marriage find their root in these passages, often interpreted through a cultural lens. I find the Fleming's linguistic re-analysis of God's words to Adam and Eve utterly compelling, life-changing, even. I cannot recommend this work highly enough."

—Leslie Leyland Fields
Author of *Crossing the Waters: Following Jesus through the Storms, the Fish, the Doubt and the Seas.*

"I've spent a significant portion of my ministry life advocating on behalf of women in our organization, and beyond, to comprehend that they are created in the image of God, purposely formed for fellowship with Him, to reflect Him to the world and to fulfill the good works for which He made them. I am always thrilled when thorough theological study confirms what I have understood. *The Book of Eden* is such a book. Bruce Fleming has crafted his wife's doctoral work into a compelling affirmation that God did not curse his first daughter, but rather assigned her to be the forerunner of our Savior and the nemesis of our enemy."

—Judy Douglass
Author of *When You Love a Prodigal*, speaker, encourager
Director, Cru Women's Resources

Table of Contents

FOREWORD

What Really Happened in the Garden of Eden?

The Book of Eden? Yes! This book is all about Genesis 2:4-3:24 where we learn about what happened in the Garden of Eden, back in the beginning. Genesis chapter 2 tells us about the creation of the human pair and God's design for marriage. Genesis chapter 3 tells us about the attack made on the couple by the serpent tempter and how each one responded.

God judged the serpent tempter and the man who rebelled against him and imposed two curses. God also responded to the woman. She hadn't willfully rebelled as did the man, but she disobeyed God by eating the forbidden fruit as had the man. God didn't curse the woman or the man. Instead, God told the woman in Line 1 of 3:16 about good news! She would have offspring who would vanquish her enemy.

People have made up many myths and stories about what supposedly happened in Eden. They make it seem like God cursed the woman and that she somehow deserved it. She didn't. They make it seem like God instituted the man's bad behavior toward his wife. God didn't.

The Bible tells us what *really* happened. And this book is all about what God really said, especially in Genesis 3:16.

PREFACE

ABOUT THIS BOOK

"Keep your finger on the text!" How did we go about researching Genesis 2:4-3:24? We made sure to "keep our finger on the text." Our professor, Dr. Walter Kaiser, always smiled when he repeatedly said this, pointing to the Hebrew text he was holding up in class. In the Bible, God communicates to us the "what" and "why" of the events that happened in the Garden of Eden. Our focus has been to communicate precisely these revealed details and to clear away the pollution that has covered over the clear meaning of the text.

Nothing herein presented should come as a surprise to students of the Hebrew text, although there likely are grammatical and theological insights they have not before considered. There is a world outside the text that we also have kept in mind. We have always kept before us the blessings and the problems of everyday life in the churches we have come to know well, in the United States, in France, and in Africa.

Our doctoral studies of the biblical text were conducted with a view to our teaching as professors at the Bangui Evangelical Graduate School of Theology in French-speaking Africa. Our findings then were shared in very diverse settings. These included being in Zaïre (now DR Congo) among the Water People, as they heard the Gospel for the very first time, and to students at the Goyongo Advanced Theological Institute in the Ubangi Province. We also shared our findings with our colleagues and taught them to our graduate students at BEST/FATEB gathered in the Central African Republic from across more than a dozen countries of Africa.

Our findings?

- That, no, God did not curse the woman, or the man.

- That the woman was not the temptress and does not deserve to be maligned.

- That the man, in fact, was a rebel in the mold of the Tempter and must be suspect in our eyes. He was the intentional eater at that Tree in the Garden and the second curse was imposed because of what *he* did.

- That God positively received the woman's truthful words and confession and she was confirmed as combatant against their Tempter.

When these chapters in Genesis are rightly understood, and we gain a true view of what God really said to the woman in Genesis 3:16, many New Testament passages can be reinvestigated. They too can be cleared away of the bias we find popping up in translations of, and commentary on, a number of key passages in the New Testament that look back to Genesis 2 and 3.

Our prayer is that translations will begin to correct their wording of Genesis 3:16. And that all throughout the church, from commentaries to preaching to hymnody, the primary colors of Eden will shine brightly.

Bruce and Joy Fleming Minneapolis 2021

The Book of Eden is based on the original eight episodes of The Eden Podcast (www.TheEdenPodcast.com), the product of many years of study on the original language and meaning of Genesis 1-3. Ground-breaking research by Dr. Joy Fleming reveals the truth long hidden by incorrect translations of Genesis 3:16. This truth corrects faulty interpretations based on those translations, which have affected countless lives over the centuries. It offers the twenty-first century church new hope in flourishing, as did the Garden of Eden back in the beginning.

Other books by Dr. Joy Fleming and Bruce C. E. Fleming include the following. They are available from the publishers and online.

 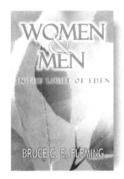 

Chapter 1

1. GENESIS 3:16 HAS BEEN POLLUTED!

 When I was a university student a major river in my home state caught fire. The flaming river was so engulfed that there were flames five-stories high coming off that river. So the fire department was called and they had to put out the river. How do you put out a body of water flowing through a city?

The problem of course wasn't just that the river itself was on fire. The problem had been that there was all kinds of pollution in the water. Hardly any fish were left alive in that river. And on top of the river all kinds of oily pollution was flowing along.

A railroad ran alongside the river at points. A passing train had sent some sparks from its wheels down into the river. It started a huge fire. It was the big story at the time. We all wondered how could a river of water catch on fire?

As people looked into it they discovered it was an ongoing problem. There had been a dozen events in previous years when that river had caught fire. Public interest in that fire moved politicians to eventually pass the Clean Water Act.

As we know today, rivers don't catch on fire. It's the pollution in the river that causes the problem. Where did the pollution come from? They went upstream to look and there they found the source of the pollution. They had to stop the pollution at its source. Then they had to clean it up all the way downstream. It took a lot of work.

I would like us to focus on Genesis 3:16, early in the Bible, because it turns out that there's been a lot of pollution dumped into that verse by translations into the modern languages we use today. They mix new ideas into the verse and cover over the ideas God put there in the original Hebrew words of the verse.

The verse itself is great. God is speaking to the woman in the Garden of Eden. But the translation of that verse has been incorrect and it's important for us to ask, "Why aren't our translations doing better?" And, "Why would there be a problem translating this verse?" "What's going on?"

Downstream from this pollution source in the Bible there have been many fires that have been lit. There are seven key passages in the Bible that talk about women and men in the home, in the church and in society that have caught on fire from this pollution. So I'd like us to think again about the Bible especially in relationship to women and men and the pollution that needs to be cleaned up in our translations to let us understand what **the pure stream of inspiration from God** is really

> *Sadly, as of right now most major translations still contain, and transmit polluted versions of Genesis 3:16!*

saying. As of right now, most major translations still contain, and transmit, that pollution.

There's been significant research done on this. During my wife's doctoral research years and afterwards she found the source of the pollution and also found that when the pollution is removed from Genesis 3:16 we see clearly what the message from God really is!

What's the pollution? Here it is. **The pollution is the idea that somehow, in some way, God basically cursed the woman in the Garden of Eden.**

Over the years, we have done informal surveys on this. We have simply asked, "How many curses did God make in the Garden of Eden?" There's a lot of confusion out there. People say that there were three curses, maybe four curses, or maybe even a lot more.

They come up with: God cursed the serpent, and God cursed the woman, and God cursed the man, oh and God cursed the ground. And some find lots more curses. But they are incorrect. God only made two curses in Eden, not three, not four and certainly not more, and importantly God never cursed the woman.

This fact pollution of excess and misplaced curses is not new. One could say it is as old as the Serpent. In ancient Jewish teachings, not in the Bible, they came up with TEN curses on Eve! They blamed them on Eve saying Eve deserved all the ten curses because supposedly, she was the problem.

Influenced by the fires set by this polluting idea, people ask questions that add to the pollution. Here's one. If she was the first woman, can we learn more about all women by studying cursed Eve? Here's another. If the first woman deserved a curse then don't all women deserve her curse?

This sounds very much like the poisonous pagan myth of Pandora. The idea there was, it was all *her* fault. All things bad came about because of her.

Who would want the world to think this way about his enemy, the woman in the Garden of Eden? All kinds of fires are started by the polluting idea that God somehow cursed the woman in the Garden of Eden.

But, the truth right from the Hebrew text of the Bible is that God did not curse the woman, or the man. God cursed only two times in the Garden

> *God cursed neither the woman, nor the man.*

of Eden. God cursed neither the woman, nor the man.

The Hebrew word for "curse" is 'arar. When God first uses the word 'arar, in Genesis 3, God curses the body of the serpent. When God uses the word 'arar the second time it is to curse the ground.

As the result of the serpent being cursed, it crawls on its belly in the dust – which is a fitting thing. The man had been made out of dust and the serpent attacked the man and the woman. Because of the curse on the serpent it would eat dust all the days of its life!

The ground also received a curse. This would change things for the woman and the man. It would cause 'itsabon which means "sorrowful-toil."

To start clearing up this pollution it is important to look at the way Genesis 2 through 3 is written out in Hebrew because the way this passage is carefully written tells us what the words themselves mean. The form of the passage itself conveys content.

> *The form of the passage conveys content.*

The very complex structure of Genesis chapters 2 and 3 was revealed by my wife, Dr. Joy Fleming, in her research. She discovered that Genesis chapters 2 through 3 contains a literary chiasm.

A chiasm. In a chiasm, early and late sections mirror each other, or have a correspondence between the first and last section, the second and the next to the last section and so on. The center section is often the key or turning point.

I find it helpful to think of a chiastic pattern kind of like a rainbow. When we see part of a rainbow going up, even though we may not see the complete rainbow coming down on the other side we know what a rainbow is like. We've seen 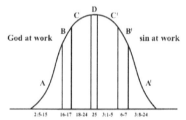 them before. And because we know that rainbows have the same colors on the way up and on the way down we can predict where the colors will end up because we know how rainbows are structured.

We need to recognize that starting with verse 4, Genesis 2-3 is structured as a chiasm, like a type of rainbow. If we note what's in the sections of Genesis chapter 2 going up we can expect certain things coming down in the sections on the other side in Genesis chapter 3.

A linchpin. My wife found another important pattern. It is the pattern in Genesis 3:15-17. This pattern links God's words to the woman with God's words to the man, and God's words to the serpent. It is an interlocking crossover pattern, or a linchpin, centered in God's words to the woman quoted in Genesis 3:16.

In time, she came across an article by a scholar who pointed out a similar linchpin pattern in the first section of Genesis chapter 2. There three verses are linked together in a similar way. This is a crucial way the sections of the chiasm in Genesis chapters 2-3 correspond to each other. There's a linchpin in the first section and there's a linchpin in the last section.

The linchpin in Genesis 3:16 is centered in God's first words to the woman. **The woman is told about two things God is going to do** that will impact her life. The first thing God will do links down to verse 17 and what God will say next to the man. The second thing links back to verse 15 and what God has just said to the serpent.

In Genesis 3:16, God says to the woman, I will greatly multiply two things. The Hebrew words for these are *'itsabon* and *heron*.

'itsabon is linked to the man's actions. God tells the woman you will have *'itsabon*. *'itsabon* means "sorrowful-toil." At this point, God doesn't tell her what will cause that to come to pass. God just says, You're going to have *'itsabon*.

But, as God talks to the man as quoted in verse 17, God tells the man, Cursed is the ground because of you and you are going to have *'itsabon*. As a result of God's cursing the ground, when the man works it with his hands he will have sorrowful-toil.

Ah! What *'itsabon* is and where it comes from becomes clear. The cause of what is prophetically spoken to the woman is revealed when God speaks to the man because this curse comes in judgment for what the man has done. *'itsabon* comes as the result of God's curse on the ground because of the man.

Curses? A lot of people think a really mean God cursed both of the human beings he made. But God didn't curse either one of them. God didn't curse either the woman or the man.

God says to the man, Cursed is ...

... the ground!

... The ground?

Not the man?

Well, that was close! God cursed the serpent. God could've cursed the man. But God didn't do that.

Here we learn more about God. God was a wonderful Creator. God created the man from dust and then the woman. The two humans were together with God in the Garden of Eden. God walked with them in the Garden, spoke to them, they had fellowship together, friendship, love. They got along well in that Garden. And now after the terrible things that happened at the beginning of Genesis chapter 3, God comes along and doesn't curse either of them!

For whatever has gone on in your life in the past and in mine, look at how wonderful God wants to be to us! God was not out to *get* either the woman or the man. And, God wants be gracious to you and to me!

So, why does God utter a second curse after cursing the serpent? God says to the man, "Cursed is the ground *because of* you." Something the man did earned that curse. God doesn't place that curse *on* the man. God *deflects* it and places that curse on the ground.

The result of the curse for the man is to be *'itsabon*, "toil," or "sorrowful-toil" when he works the soil with his hands.

This Hebrew word *'itsabon* is used only three times in the Bible. It is not a general word that can be taken in various ways. It is only used in regard to the ground the Lord God curses. It is not used any other time in any other place to mean anything else except the sorrowful toil that will come from working the cursed ground doing fieldwork.

The only other time *'itsabon* is used in the Bible, besides Genesis 3:16 and 3:17, is in Genesis 5:29. There, the father of Noah (there's a familiar name, we all know about Noah and the Flood) Noah's father gives us additional insight into this sorrowful toil and how it is affecting everyone. The child is named "Noah" which means "relief" or "comfort," and here is the verse: "This one, Noah, will comfort us concerning our work and the sorrowful toil, 'itsabon, of our hands, because of the ground which the Lord has cursed."

Two other Hebrew words that sound similar to 'itsabon are used in the context of Genesis 3. They are 'ets which is the word for tree and 'etsev which means effort. Neither one has to do with the specific heartbreaking sorrowful-toil of 'itsabon that is used only these three times in the Bible and only when talking about working the ground God curses because of the man. This sorrowful-toil God tells the woman about in Genesis 3:16 is not something that applies only to the woman. She will experience it at the same time the man will experience it when they work the fields.

We can now translate together what God says to the woman in Genesis 3:16:

I'm going to greatly multiply your 'itsabon, your sorrowful toil, in fieldwork.

In 3:16, the word "and" introduces the second thing that God will multiply. It is this: and, I'm going to multiply your *heron. Heron* is the Hebrew word for "pregnancy" or even "conception." This is good news!

In Genesis chapter 1, at the end of the chapter, God *blesses* the man and the woman. And God tells them to "Be fruitful and multiply." There's that word – "multiply!" The woman hears it when God speaks to them at creation telling them to "multiply." There the word is linked with blessing, with multiple children. It is a wonderful word.

If you look elsewhere in the Old Testament in addition to Genesis 3:16 you'll find the words "multiplying I will multiply" used two more times in the same specific grammatical construction that is used in Genesis 3:16. Both refer to Abraham's offspring. God will multiply his offspring so that they will be as numerous as the sands on the seashore, or as numerous as the stars of the heavens.

In Genesis 3:16 God says, I'm going to multiply your toil, your sorrowful toil, your 'itsabon. Then God wonderfully adds a good thing, I'm going to multiply your *heron.* I'm going to greatly multiply your pregnancies.

Multiplied *heron*, pregnancy or conception, is good news. This is God confirming they will be carrying out their mandate to be fruitful and multiply. Also, this involves God's announcing a coming Messiah!

To summarize, God tells the woman, I will greatly multiply two things – a bad thing and a good thing. First, the bad thing is you will have sorrowful toil in cultivating with your hands the ground which is about to be cursed. Second, the good thing is you're going to have *heron*, multiplied pregnancies.

Mistranslations! But, if you look in your Bible you likely won't read about *these two things* God tells the woman. Instead you'll come across a very different thing, a *single idea* that sounds almost like a curse! And a lot of people take it that way.

Here's the way three of the most widespread versions have put it (and most of the others sound the same note). The way they word their mistranslation of the verse alters the meaning and makes it sound very different from the actual Hebrew text. They say, you're going to have one new very bad thing at the very end of your pregnancy.

HCSB - "I will intensify your labor pains;"
ESV - "I will surely multiply your pain in childbearing,"
NASB - "Surely I will multiply your pain in childbirth,"

Put this way they've completely covered over God's word about her having "sorrowful toil" in field work just like the man will have! Put this way, they've changed God's word to her about her promised "pregnancies" to focus on only the very end of the nine month process. They miss the point here that God will be the agent in giving her children.

According to the Hebrew words these versions are supposed to be translating, God clearly spoke two words to her and joined them together with an "and." But these mistranslations have covered over these two words with word pollution!

The second thing God promises to multiply is "pregnancy," or "conception." That word must be clearly stated in our translations because it is linked in the linchpin to the word "offspring" or "seed" (*zera'* in Hebrew) that God uses in Genesis 3:15.

There God speaks to the serpent and tells the serpent:

You know, you've got problems coming! I heard what the woman just said. And her words were true. You lied to her and deceived her and she's just revealed your actions. I'm confirming her and you as combatants. You're going to strike at her offspring's heel. But her offspring is going to Crush. Your. Head.

We'll come back to this and go more in depth. We'll also look at why translations have gone astray. Right now, at this point, as we think again about the cosmic battle being waged by the serpent against the woman and against the meaning of God's words to her in our translations, we need to clear up the pollution covering over Genesis 3:16. **We need to restore the pure stream of inspiration from God. We need a true 3:16.**

Study Guide 1

STUDY: AN OVERVIEW OF GENESIS 3:16

Genesis 3:16 has been polluted!

A major river caught fire in 1969. The source of the pollution came from upstream. It was found and corrected. The Clean Water Act was passed to fight further pollution.

In the same way, Genesis 3:16 has been polluted. The Tru316 Project (Tru316.com) has been launched to clean up the word pollution of Genesis 3:16 and seven related passages:

1. Genesis 2
2. Genesis 3
3. Ephesians 5:15-6:9
4. 1 Timothy 2:8-3:13
5. 1 Corinthians 11:2-16
6. 1 Corinthians 14:34-40
7. 1 Peter 3:1-7

Exercise #1: Identify the main doctrine or teaching you are familiar with for each passage listed above.

How does each doctrine link back to Genesis 3:16?

1.

2.

3.

4.

5.

6.

7.

Exercise #2: Why don't our translations do better?

1. *Read Genesis 3:9-12.*
   a. Which questions does the man answer? Which does he avoid?

   Why?

   b. Who does the man name in his answer? Who does he not name?

   Why?

   c. How might John 3:20 and John 8:44 with Genesis 3:15 provide insight into the man's behavior and answer?

   d. How does the man's answer reveal his new loyalties?

2. *Read Genesis 3:13-16.*
   a. How thoroughly did the woman answer God's question?

   b. How are the woman's loyalties revealed in her answer?

c. How might the woman's loyalties and God's words to her in Genesis 3:16 be related?

3. *Read Genesis 2:25.*

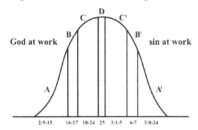

Genesis 2-3 is formed as a chiasm. Genesis 2:5-24 is the upward curve of God at work, and Genesis 3:1-24 is the downward curve of sin at work. Genesis 2:25 is at the summit. Compare the two sides of this chiasm. *What do you see?*

a. Compare Genesis 2:5-15 with Genesis 3:8-24 (A and A')

b. Compare Genesis 2:16-17 with Genesis 3:6-7 (B and B')

c. Compare Genesis 2:18-24 with Genesis 3:1-5 (C and C')

d. How does Genesis 2:25 act as the summit? (D)

First, God tells the woman of *two* certain actions.
One *links down* to the curse on the ground because of the man
(verse 16 *'itsabon* ⟶ verse 17 *'itsabon*).
One *links back* to the promise of the birth of Offspring who will crush the tempter
(verse 15 *zera'* ⟵ verse 16 *heron*).

Genesis 3:16 (Line 1) **I will surely multiply (1) your sorrowful toil in fieldwork *and* (2) your conception.**

Then, God instructs the woman about what has happened, to her and to them, now that they are mortal and fallen.

(Line 2) **With effort you will bring forth children**
(Line 3) **Your [loving] desire [is] to your husband**
(Line 4) **But he [is rebelliously ruling over himself and] will rule over you.**

The first four Hebrew words spoken to the woman in Genesis 3:16 are:

(word #1) **Multiplying (*harbah*)**
(word #2) **I-will-multiply ('*arbeh*)**
(word #3) **Your-sorrowful-toil (in fieldwork) ('*itsabon*)**

This Hebrew word links down to the exact same word spoken to the man in verse 17.

(word #4) **And-your-conception (*heron*)**

This Hebrew word links back to the word seed/offspring in verse 15.

> v. 15 ...Between your seed and her <u>seed</u>
> He shall bruise you on the head
> and you shall bruise him on the heel.
> v. 16 I will greatly multiply...your <u>conception</u>
>
> v. 16 I will greatly multiply...your <u>toil</u> ...
>
> v. 17 Cursed is the ground ... In <u>toil</u> you shall eat of it

Yet, modern translations pollute words #3 ('*itsabon*) and #4 (*heron*) by covering them over with *one* very different and incorrect idea which is equivalent to a curse: **your pain in childbearing**

Exercise #3: Understand God's word to the woman in light of a true translation.

1. In Genesis 3:16:
   a. Which part gives God's actions, and what will God now do?

   b. What part gives God's explanation, and what is explained?

2. From the translation below, how is your understanding of God's pronouncement to the woman affected when reading the true translation?

Genesis 3:15-17

15 "I will put enmity between you and the woman,
   and between your offspring and **her-offspring**;
   he will bruise you on the head,
   and you will bruise him on the heel."

16 To the woman he said,
   (Line 1) "I will greatly multiply *your-sorrowful-toil* **and-your-conception**;
   (Line 2) with-effort you-will-give-birth-to children.
   (Line 3) Your affection is for your husband
   (Line 4) but he will rule over you."

17 And to the man he said,
   "Because you listened to the voice of your wife and ate from the tree
   About which I commanded you, saying, 'You shall not eat of it,'
   cursed is the ground because of you;
   in *sorrowful-toil* you will eat of it all the days of your life."

Chapter 2

2. GENESIS 2:18, EQUAL PARTNERS

In Chapter 1 we took our first look at the terrible problems caused by the word pollution modern translations of the Bible have been pouring into Genesis 3:16. And we looked into some of the problems this has caused. Starting with this chapter, we will go back into Genesis chapter 2 and look into one of the fires that has been started by the backwash of the theological pollution that has been caused by incorrect understandings of the Hebrew text of Genesis 3:16. We will work our way from Genesis 2:18 through to the end of Genesis 3 and God's chasing out the man from the Garden of Eden back in the beginning.

Have you noticed? There are some Bible verses that stand out. They seem to touch everyone and change everything. Genesis 3:16 is one of these verses. Genesis 2:18 is another.

Sadly, mistranslations and misinterpretations of Genesis 3:16 have led to misleading and even harmful teachings from what many mistakenly think is found in the first chapters of Genesis.

Later passages in the Bible might tell of a certain king here, or a certain shipwreck there. But the first chapters in Genesis, and especially Genesis 2-3, are packed full of meaning. They explain why our world is a mixture of good and evil. They even reveal the roots of the titanic spiritual battles we are experiencing.

Let me tell you the story of how Joy and I came to focus specifically on Genesis 3:16 and the passages related to it like 2:18. When we were preparing to teach in Africa, we were interviewed by African leaders who gave us this advice. "Don't do your doctoral research on something you think might be interesting but may turn out to be of little help to us here. First, find out what the people of Africa need to know from the Bible. Do your research on that. Then, you'll be a real help to us."

Since we both would be serving as missionary professors in French-speaking Africa, we spent two years in France learning the language. Our first year, we attended advanced language school in the French Alps.

Our second year, we perfected our French by using it doing doctoral studies. Joy studied Old Testament. I studied Practical Theology. It was the first time the University of Strasbourg School of Theology had a wife and husband duo with each studying in a doctoral program of theology at the same time.

Joy focused on Genesis 2-3, having been advised that such studies would be quite useful in Africa. She would be able to study the Beginning, the person of God, Man and Woman, Sin, Death and Curses. I studied the New Testament and Contextualization of Theology in Africa.

Then we headed for Africa. Sometime after the birth of our daughter and moving to a nearby population center and settling in to our home, we were robbed! All the course notes I had taken down during class lectures and the notes from my research in the libraries in France were stolen. The thieves apparently thought my metal portable filing box was a strong box for valuables.

Valuables? When they saw only papers inside they got rid of them and just kept the box. Apparently, they sold some of the papers to be used in the marketplace for wrapping fish!

What could I do next? I couldn't leave Africa to go back to Europe to retake my doctoral seminars. There had been a changeover in professors at the University. And each year different subjects were being offered at that level. We felt the loss deeply. All that work was gone – to the fish!

For months we prayed, "God, is there any way to bring good out of this evil?" Was it somehow possible to pick up my studies and go on? Was there something else God wanted me to study? The answer came a year later when we moved deep into the rainforest to teach in a small theological institute.

There, out our front door, down the hill, under the dark green shade of towering avocado trees, past the end of the grass airstrip and then the whitewashed clinic, came the end of the mile-long dirt path. From that point you could only turn right or left down the main road, which was only a one-lane rutted track, crowded on both sides by thick rainforest.

To the right, you came to the first mud-walled, thatched-roof huts in a line of villages that belonged to people from the Mono tribe. To the left, you soon found a larger village. These people were from the Ngombe tribe. Their villages lined the mud road away to the west. In this juxtaposition of culture groups, in the lush hills of northwestern Congo, Joy and I took turns raising our toddler daughter and teaching courses to students who were preparing for pastoral work in village churches in the Congo.

The initial coming of Christianity to new culture groups anywhere in the world almost always results in a marked improvement in the status of women in those groups. To my surprise, I found that after 25 years of mission work and church planting, the status of women had *not* improved in the Mono and Ngombe villages that lined the Bosobolo Road. In fact, their lowly status in the two tribes remained remarkably as it had been before the arrival of the Gospel in their area. Why?

As a Practical Theologian, I began digging to find what had been taught, and what had not been taught by the first missionaries and African pastors. What had been done right? What had been misunderstood? What had been done wrong?

I interviewed older believers in their villages and took notes. I searched the school library, the archives and the shelves in the various offices. My searching paid off, as I found on a top shelf many dust-covered, yellowing booklets that had been used in Bible and Practical Christian Life training during the early years in the school.

I discovered that incorrect doctrine had inadvertently been taught in the village churches. This was hindering the growth of the Christian women and men in their faith and their ministry. It was disrupting their home life as well!

Many of these incorrect teachings were based on misinterpretations of Genesis 2-3. Additional faulty teachings, based on these misinterpretations of Genesis warped the understanding of key New Testament passages as well. I realized that here was the Biblical research and writing God had for me to do.

As Joy and I each tackled tough passages, we noted faulty translations into modern languages from the Hebrew Old Testament and the Greek New Testament in seven key passages. Working from the original languages, we began to peel away centuries of faulty interpretation and arrived at clear expressions of the passages we were studying.

We taught what we learned to the students and believers around us. It was a privilege to see their troubled expressions turn to ones of recognition and joy as the Bible studies progressed.

Since then, we have continued to study and teach on the seven passages which build on the insights Joy discovered in Genesis 3:16. These are the seven passages:

Genesis 2,
Genesis 3,
Ephesians 5:15-6:9,
1 Timothy 1:18-3:13,
1 Corinthians 11:2-16,
1 Corinthians 14:34-40 and
1 Peter 3:1-7.

"In the beginning, God." In Genesis 1:1, on Day One of Creation, the name used for God in Hebrew (*Elohim*) ends with "-*im*." That was like ending an English name with the letter "-*s*." The "-*im*" ending usually meant "more than one." But there was only one God "in the beginning."

A careful look at the first chapter of Genesis shows that God Three-in-One was at work "in the beginning." Verses 1-3 could be worded this way:

Verse 1: ... the Father Three-in-One created the heavens and the earth.

Verse 2: ... the Spirit Three-in-One hovered over the waters.

Verse 3: ... the Word Three-in-One said, "Let there be light...."

This fits the description of what happened on Day Six of Creation:

Verse 26: ... God Three-in-One said, Let us make humans, male and female, in our image, in our likeness, and let them rule ...

Verse 28: ... God Three-in-One blessed the man and woman and said to them, Be fruitful and multiply; fill the earth and subdue it. Rule over the fish of the sea and the birds of the air and over every living creature that moves on the ground.

Thus, according to Genesis 1, on Day Six of Creation:

Both the man and the woman were made in God's image (1:27).
Both the woman and the man were given the creation mandate to multiply and fill the earth (1:27).
Both were made as rulers. (1:28)
And, all was very good (1:31).

Now let's look at the details of Day Six in Genesis 2. What is summarized in Genesis 1 is told with details in Genesis 2:4-25. Genesis 2 describes what happens on Day Six of Creation when God specially creates each of our first parents and they begin life with the Lord God in the Garden of Eden.

The Lord God forms the man from the dust of the ground. After God breathes into him the breath of life, the man meets God (2:7). Then the Lord God plants a Garden in Eden and places the man in it (2:8-15).

The fruit from all the trees can be enjoyed, but the fruit from the Tree of the Knowledge of Good and Evil is not to be eaten. The penalty for eating from the forbidden Tree is death (16-17).

Then, Genesis 2 tells of the creation of the woman. The Lord God makes an assessment, "It is not good for the man to be alone. I will make a partner corresponding to him" (2:18).

What was not good? Five times the word "good" is used up to this point in Creation. What is "not good?" A look at the end of Day Five provides the insight we need.

At that point God blesses the recently made birds of the air and creatures of the water with these words, "Be fruitful and multiply..." (1:22). A similar blessing is coming for the man and woman at the end of Day Six (1:28). But at this point on Day Six the man is alone. He cannot be blessed to reproduce as it takes a male and a female to do so.

I think he was aware that he was a *male* human. He had named the animals. When he named the lions, for example he likely observed there were male and female lions with their physical differences. The same would have been true for other animals. But where was the *female* human? Creation was obviously incomplete.

Readers of Genesis 2 have the delightful experience of listening to God talking within the Trinity, so to speak. Here's a playful yet respectful way to sum up what we read next.

"On Day Five we blessed the birds and the fish to be fruitful and multiply. We can't do the Day Six blessing yet because we don't have the last piece of the puzzle. All is not good, yet. That is the state of affairs so far. Let us finish this and give the man insight into what we're doing. Yes. That'll be great. We're starting to fellowship with the first of all of them already. When we're done all will be very good!" (2:18; 1:31).

How did the Lord God make the woman? There are different descriptive verbs used when each person is made. God "forms" the man from the ground (2:7). God "builds" the woman from the already existing material taken from the man (2:22).

Created to be equal partners. In Genesis 2, when God creates the woman, she is described in relation to the man. In two Hebrew words packed full of meaning, *'ezer kenegdo*, God describes how the two are designed to go together. They are made for each other, just hours apart. Once together, they are to be a resourceful and satisfied pair, at home together in Eden.

Modern language versions of the Bible translate these two Hebrew words in confusing and contradictory ways. But there really is no cause for confusion. The two words in Genesis 2:18 are not that hard to translate.

An *'ezer kenegdo* is someone who is equal, a counterpart, one who works together with another as they help each other through sharing their strengths.

As for the Hebrew word *'ezer*:

The majority of times it is used in the Bible, it is used to describe *God*. In Deuteronomy 33:7, God is the *'ezer* of Judah. The NIV translates this as: "Oh, be his *help* against his foes." God is the *'ezer* who *helps* with superior strength.

The Bible also uses *'ezer* to describe one king who *helps* another as allies in battle. The word *'ezer* refers to someone on the same level who helps by sharing his strength with another (as Pharaoh in Isaiah 30:1-5).

As for the word *kenegdo*:

This word creates a picture of two people facing each other. It can be translated as "vis-à-vis," "conspicuously facing," "corresponding to" or "equal to."

Further studies in the Hebrew use of the word *kenegdo* outside of the Bible by Michael Rosenzweig[1] show that those who were in that kind of relationship were partners. He translates *'ezer kenegdo* as "equal partners." It takes two to be partners. Both the man and the woman are equal partners with each other. Both are involved in an equal partnership.

---

[1] Michael L. Rosenzweig, "A Helper Equal to Him," *Judaism* 35/3 (1968): 277-80.

Many couples don't live together this way. And we wonder why our lives don't work out as well as the relationship Adam and Eve had when they first started out in Eden.

The woman is *'ezer kenegdo* to the man. Thus, she is a corresponding ally or a partner equal with the man.

Sadly, *this* is not what had been taught along the Bosobolo Road in Congo for so many years. And it showed. Women were on a level little higher than domesticated animals! There seemed to be little restraint to the practice of polygamy. We began teaching what the Bible really says, that wives and husbands were created by God to be equal partners, and trusted God to work in the lives of the couples in those local churches.

Even correcting the errors in Genesis chapter 2 would turn out not to be enough. Keeping women in a low and unequal status in the home, in their cultural practices and in the church was perpetuated by incorrect teaching on the content and meaning of Genesis 3:16. **They needed the true meaning of 3:16.**

Study Guide 2

STUDY: *'ezer kenegdo*

Though the status of women almost always improves with the introduction of Christianity to a new culture group, this had *not* happened in the Mono and Ngombe villages along the Bosobolo Road in NW DR Congo. Even after twenty-five years.

Why not? *Because the foundation of their Christian education included incorrect doctrine that hindered growth of faith and ministry.*

A *mis*reading of Genesis 3:16 led to a misreading of Genesis 1:26-28 and 2:18-25.

This Chapter's study guide touches on the Christian understanding of God as God-Three-in-One. Each person of the Godhead is unique and acts in unique ways yet is also one with the other persons. Each person of the Godhead is also fully God, fully infinite, eternal, and equal in being. Each person of God-Three-in-One shares the same essence, attributes, power, glory, and authority.

Exercise #1: Develop a correct understanding of God's creative acts in Genesis 1.

   1.   *Read Genesis 1:1-3.* In each verse, describe which Person of God-Three-in-One is being portrayed:

Verse 1

Verse 2

Verse 3 (for help, see John 1:1-3)

2. *Read Genesis 1:26-31.*
    a. How is *Elohim* portrayed in the word "our"?

    b. God made the first **man**,

        •   In whose image? (1:27)

        •   With what mandate? (1:27-28)

        •   With what summation? (1:31)

    c. God made first **woman**,

        •   In whose image? (1:27)

        •   With what mandate? (1:27-28)

        •   With what summation? (1:31)

3. According to Genesis 1:26a, how might man and woman be in the image of God-Three-in-One?

Genesis 2:4-25 focuses in on Day Six of creation. We see God forming the man, planting the Garden, giving instruction, explaining about the two Trees in the Garden, and fashioning the woman.

When God creates the woman, she is described in relation to the man. In two Hebrew words packed full of meaning, *'ezer kenegdo*, God describes how the two are designed to go together. They are equal partners made for each other, and once together, they are to be a resourceful and satisfied pair, at home together in Eden.

Exercise #2: Build on what we know from Genesis 1 with details we learn in Genesis 2.

1. *Read several translations of Genesis 2:18-25.* (Free online Bible apps such as Bible Gateway and Bible Hub enable you to find other translations.)

   a. Survey Genesis 1. How often is the word "good" spoken by God?

   b. What is "not good" in Genesis 2?

   c. Compare Genesis 1:22 and 1:28 with the man's condition in Genesis 2:18, and explain what God meant by "not good."

2. Using a Hebrew-English lexicon, if possible, define the Hebrew words

   a. *'ezer*

   b. *kenegdo*

3. How is *'ezer* portrayed in each of the following Bible passages? *Example:* Exodus 18:4. The **God** of my father was my ***help*** and **delivered** me....
   Deuteronomy 33:7, 26, 29

   Psalm 33:20

   Psalm 70:5

   Psalm 89:19

   Psalm 115:10-11

   Psalm 121:1-2

   Psalm 124:8

   Daniel 11:34

   Hosea 13:9

Further studies in the Hebrew use of the word *kenegdo* by Rosenzweig show that those who are in this kind of relationship are partners. **He** translates *'ezer kenegdo* as **"equal partners."** It takes two to be partners. Both are involved in an equal partnership.

    4. Characterize the woman God made, and the relationship she was to share with the man.

Notice that the direction we took in learning about the human beings God made: we moved forward in the narration, from Genesis 1 to Genesis 2. However, many scholars move *backward* in the narration from Genesis 3 *back* to Genesis 2, which leads to problems.

Exercise #3: Trace the *backflow* of a wrong translation and interpretation of Genesis 3:16 to a wrong translation of Genesis 2:18.

    1. Compare Genesis 2:18 in several Bible translations.

       a. What words are used to translate *'ezer kenegdo*?

       b. How is the ideal relationship between the man and the woman typically described—as equal, or unequal with one of them requiring a leader?

    2. Because of the incorrect perception that God cursed the first woman in Genesis 3:16, explain how Genesis 2:18 has been mistranslated and misinterpreted.

    3. How have these incorrect ideas touched the everyday lives of people in your culture?

Review: The correct translation of Genesis 3:15-17

Genesis 3:15-17

15 "I will put enmity between you and the woman,
    and between your offspring and **her-offspring**;
    he will bruise you on the head,
    and you will bruise him on the heel."
16 To the woman he said,
    (Line 1) "I will greatly multiply ***your-sorrowful-toil* and-your-
    conception**;

(Line 2) with-effort you-will-give-birth-to children.
(Line 3) Your affection [is] for your husband
(Line 4) but he will rule over you."

17 And to the man he said,

"Because you listened the voice of your wife and ate from the tree
About which I commanded you, saying, 'You shall not eat of it,'
cursed is the ground because of you;
in **sorrowful-toil** you will eat of it all the days of your life."

Review: The correct translation of Genesis 2:18

Then the Lord God said, "It is not good for the man to be alone; I will make a partner equal with him."

Chapter 3

3. GENESIS 2:21-25, MARRIAGE MODEL

While my wife Joy and I were doing our doctoral studies in theology in Strasbourg, France, I gained access to a centuries-old Bible that had been used by John Calvin.

That Bible is very different from modern Bibles in the way it is laid out on the page. There are no verse numbers. Instead, in the left and right side margins there are the letters A, B, C and D to set off each quarter of the page. That's not all that I found strange. In a copy of Calvin's *Commentaries*, I saw he had misinterpreted the Hebrew word, *'ezer*, in Genesis 2:18 that means "partner."

How could he have done *that*? Calvin was a reformer of the false doctrines and practices that had grown up over the centuries within the late medieval Church. He managed to address, and set right, many things. But not everything.

The Roman Catholic theologians of his day operated in a world of hierarchies in the church and in the home. Like these theologians, John Calvin promoted the false doctrine that woman had been created to be subservient to man; she had been created to be the man's junior partner. I was surprised to read Calvin's comment on Genesis 2:18. He described the woman as being "like a cook's helper."

Calvin's incorrect understanding of the meaning of the Hebrew word *'ezer* was passed on to his followers. The results of this fundamental mistake gave a false tilt to much of the rest of the theology he wrote. This incorrect theology persists among many of his adherents to this day. But it must not stand!

In the Garden of Eden, when the Lord puts the man into a deep sleep and makes the woman from his side, she takes her first breath and meets God. The man is asleep. The man and the woman each know the companionship of God before they meet each other.

After that, God introduces and marries the man and the woman. Then, they both know the one-flesh companionship of one another. Genesis 2:24-25 describes their wonderful relationship in the presence of God: "... a man shall ... be joined to his wife; and they shall become one flesh. ... the man and his wife were both naked and were not ashamed."

From Genesis chapter 2, when the man and woman were in their ideal situation in the presence of the Lord God their creator, we gain a very complete description of what God had in mind for marriage. And how God had in mind that a man and a woman in any and all of the later generations after Adam and Eve should marry. These verses are very important for the understanding of what marriage is and how God intended we get married is a very fuzzy idea in the minds of many people.

A wedding in Africa. Let me tell of an experience I had that drove me to study these verses in Genesis 2 more closely. One weekend, in Africa, I went for one ceremony but attended two. Seven students were going to graduate the next day from a small two-year Bible school in the rain forest on the banks of the Ubangi River in NW DR Congo. It was a good Bible school. All involved were dear believers in the body of Christ.

I had been specially flown there in a small plane to be the speaker at their graduation ceremony the next day. There were six men and one woman who would receive their diplomas. But first they had another ceremony to attend, and that one surprised me.

Not long after we landed in the late afternoon, the pilot and I were invited to walk up to the local church that doubled as a chapel building to attend a wedding ceremony. Into the church in slow procession walked all seven students dressed in Western fashion to get married.

There were six couples in all. It was pointed out to me that among the 12 people who filed into the church there were the seven graduating students. Five of the students had brides who were not students. And two of the students would marry each other.

The couples happily stood up front, ready to be *married*. There they gathered, along with their many children! Some of them were six or seven years old. Perhaps I was utterly naïve but I was totally confused.

I tentatively asked the dignitary next to me if this was the regular practice of their churches. "Oh yes! Before their graduation ceremonies from Bible school the prospective graduates take part in a Christian marriage, white dresses and all." To my eyes, these couples obviously had been *united* long before this ceremony.

Why did they do it? I asked. "Oh, they want to start their ministry careers having church-recognized Christian unions." That was good intent. But somehow, I reasoned it was preferable for their unions to have been recognized by their families and their churches long before their relationships had gotten this far.

Later the next day, I was winging my way over the rainforest, returning to my wife and child. We had gotten married in an obviously Western ceremony too. That's when I doubled down to look for the ideal pattern from Eden for any and all marriages.

Man *and* woman. In Genesis 2:18, God observes that something is "not good," in other words, the man is alone. So God will make another human. They will be a matched pair.

In Genesis 2:19-20, it is observed that there is no counterpart to the man to be found among the animals, even though they are created beings which are somewhat similar (also made from the ground) but different from him (they do not have the divine breath of life). The man recognizes that he is unique and alone as a human being.

In verses 21-22, God creates a corresponding human being, but not from dust. Woman is specially and carefully made by God's hands, created from the very material of man.

She is the resolution to the situation that was "not good." In 2:23, the man joyfully recognizes that she appropriately corresponds to him and that she is the companion he was without. He is the *male* human, the Hebrew word is *'ish* and she is the female human, the Hebrew word is *'ishshah*. God's work reaches completion with her creation. She is the pinnacle of God's creative work.

The ideal pattern. This first marriage, and the description of marriages to come, is the ideal pattern for all men and women to follow. I found the pattern has four points. I started out with just the last three, but then I realized that there are four points to the marriage model in Genesis 2.

1. Each member of the union to be, separately, knows God personally.
2. The man leaves his birth family and together with his wife they establish a new family unit. His primary allegiance is no longer to his parents but to her.
3. When the man leaves his parents to join his wife, his parents and all in his local society are put on notice that here is a new family unit.
4. Because they are joined together in the presence of God, the church, the body of believers, recognizes their new family unit.

Let's look into these four points a bit more.

First, each member of the union to be, separately, knows God personally. In the beginning, when the man opens his eyes for the first time he knows God and is known by God. In the beginning, when the woman opens her eyes for the first time she knows God and is known by God. Each knows God in a personal and lively way.

This should be very easy but it's very hard for *us* to consider in a world filled with rebellion and death.

We might ask, well, are they Christians? Or at least, do they know God in the way that an Old Testament believer knows God? The short answer is yes. Yes, they do. Each is in a perfect relationship with God, knowing God.

In this sense, we have two believers in God who will be coming together in marriage. This is the ideal. To first know God and then, when it comes to marriage, to join together with another believer in God.

Second, the man leaves his birth family and together with his wife they establish a new family unit. His primary allegiance is to her.

The Hebrew word for "to-leave" is *azav*. It can carry the meaning of "to abandon." First, the man is the one who is the "abandoner." He is the one who "forsakes" and "leaves" his own family unit. Such "abandoning" or desertion "of his father and mother" is observed and recognized by others. Reciprocal action on the woman's part is not required.

In the Garden of Eden there was nobody else around. And nobody had parents yet. Verse 2:24 is referring to everybody else after the first man and woman, who had no parents. The man's marriage is to be a public affair. His family and the rest of society with them all know that the man is leaving his parents.

In cultures around the world when there is a moment when all recognize that here is the beginning of the life of a new family unit they are following the example set down in Genesis 2. When such a beginning is not clearly established, when an intimate relationship is started between a man and a woman without a publicly recognized launching point, people are not following the ideal pattern from Eden.

I encountered this as a practical issue where - I'll call them - trial marriages were practiced. A new family unit was not publicly acknowledged, for example, until a first child was produced. Or perhaps until two or three had been born and had survived early childhood. This is not in the pattern from Eden. What if there never is a child produced? What is their relationship then?

Churches lived in confusion. No church wedding had been held. No cultural ceremony had been held either. The parents had not definitively been left by the man. Yet here was a couple living together. Were they married? Was the woman to be recognized as a wife of a certain man? Was that man considered to be married at all?

Third, the next part of the ideal pattern is that the man "cleaves," "clings," or "keeps close" (the Hebrew word is *dabaq*) to his woman. The verb expresses strong attachment in personal loyalty and commitment.

The same verb is used in Ruth 1:14 where Ruth clings to her mother-in-law. Not wanting to part, Ruth adopts the people of Israel, her mother-in-law's people, as her own.

Here, the man's devotion, affection and allegiance changes from two parents to one woman. He becomes loyal to her above all others. The expression "his woman" is not to imply possession or ownership, but rather expresses the exclusivity of the marriage commitment. The loyalty and strong emotional attachment of marriage are designed exclusively for one man and one woman.

Fourth, the final part of the pattern involves both the man and the woman who in concert "become one flesh." Physical union consummates the marriage. With these four points in the pattern from Genesis 2 a couple is married. There is no need for a Western-style ceremony years later.

But don't they have to get married western-style, with a white dress for the bride and a formal church wedding? No, they don't. But these are serious questions in non-Western cultures.

Adam and Eve didn't wear formal clothes to their wedding. They wore no clothes at all. They had no church building to get married in. They had no buildings. Yet their marriage is fully a model for all ages and cultures.

At the creation when God builds the woman from part of the man, what has been one, becomes two. Then, in marriage what is formerly two becomes one. When the words "one flesh" are used, "flesh" emphasizes the physical; "one" emphasizes their oneness or their unity. This Hebrew word for "one" stands for a unity with different parts.

It's the word that is used in Deuteronomy 6:4. There it is written, "Hear, O Israel! The LORD is our God, the Lord is ONE."

In some countries, for various reasons, up to 25% of a population may be unable to have children. According to traditional cultures, these marriages are incomplete. They are not valid marriages. It is possible to dismiss a so-called barren spouse, or one can add an additional spouse in order to have children.

But even though the first couple was blessed by God to be fruitful and multiply, having children was not listed as a necessary part of creating a successful new family unit for those who would be married after them.

The fact that Genesis 2 does not contain any requirement to have children was *not* communicated to the villagers in Congo where my wife and I used to work. As a result, church members were still breaking up, or re-ordering, their Christian family units. We have to learn the expectations of each local culture and point out what the Bible requires and does not require of us in a Christian home.

In the beginning, God could have made the two humans simultaneously from dust. But God chose instead to make one from the other, underlining their common essence. God could not have made that point more effectively. And marriage underscores this fact once again. God took one and made two. In marriage, two join to become one.

Genesis chapters 2 and 3 is written out in the structure of a chiasm, which is like a rainbow. The high point of it all comes in what came to be numbered as verse 25 of chapter 2.

In verse 25, creation is complete. God has made a beautiful world. There is completion and harmony in all realms. Verse 25 sums up the situation regarding the man and the woman. They were naked and not ashamed.

Some people add to what Genesis tells us about the beginning. They take what happened later on in our sinful history and project that back into the Garden of Eden. I'm sure you've come across this. I'm thinking specifically of the ideas of "hierarchy" and "authority."

In the beginning in Genesis up to this point, God makes only two references to human relationships that involve authority.

First, *God* has authority and rules over humans in all that God commands and instructs, and God prohibits one tree from consumption. This is not to trap or trip up the man and woman. Rather, it serves a positive function for it is a visible reminder of their dependence on their Creator. By their obedience, they acknowledge God's governing right in their lives. By their disobedience, they would declare their independence from God.

Second, one other authority structure is clearly spelled out. God tells man and woman to subdue the earth and to have dominion over its animal inhabitants (1:26).

Conspicuously absent in Genesis 1-2 is any advice or command from God for man to exercise authority over woman. This is such an important subject that had such an authority structure been part of the creation design, God would have clearly stated it along with the two other ruling relationships. The total absence of such a commission indicates that it was not part of God's intent.

The two partners complement one another. Their relationship is characterized by mutuality as they live harmoniously with each other as equal partners. And each lives in communion with the Creator, the superior of them both.

Only God was in authority over Adam and Eve. Neither of them had the right to usurp God's rulership rights over either of them. Any teaching that inserts an authority structure between Adam and Eve in God's creation design is to be firmly rejected since it is not founded on the biblical text.

[John   Calvin | Pixabay.com

Study Guide 3

STUDY: GENESIS MARRIAGE MODEL

While my wife Joy and I were doing our doctoral studies in Strasbourg, France, I gained access to a centuries-old copy of the translation John Calvin used of the Bible into French. In a copy of Calvin's *Commentaries*, I saw that **Calvin had *misinterpreted* the word in Genesis 2:18** that means "partner," or "help," and described the woman as being "like a cook's helper." He held to the false doctrine that woman had been created to be subservient to man.

This Chapter's study focuses on God's marriage of the man and woman and what God had in mind for marriage.

Exercise #1: Establish what God was revealing to the man about an ideal counterpart.

1. *Read Genesis 2:7, 15, 18-20.* What did the man observe about the animals and birds that showed him he was unique and alone as a human being?

2. *Read Genesis 2:21-22.* Why do you think God made the woman in this way? How do the following passages help explain God's intention?

a.   Genesis 1:1-3

b.   Genesis 2:23

c.   Genesis 2:24

d.   Deuteronomy 6:4

e.   John 1:1-3

f.   John 10:30

g.   John 17:11

h.   Ephesians 5:31-32

The ideal pattern. This first marriage, and the description of marriages to come, is the ideal pattern for all men and women to follow, a pattern with four points:

1.   Each member of the union to be, separately, *knows God personally.*
2.   The man *leaves his birth family* and together with his wife they establish a new family unit. His primary allegiance is no longer to his parents but to her.
3.   When the man leaves his parents to join his wife, his parents and *all society* is put on notice that here is a *new family unit.*
4.   Because they are joined together in the presence of God, the church, *the body of believers, recognizes* their new family unit.

Exercise #2: Understand "to-leave"—*azav*—and "cleaves"—*dabaq.*

1.   How does Ruth 1:16-17 shed light on what is involved in "to-leave"?

2.   From Joshua 22:5 and Ruth 1:14 describe "cleaves."

3. Remembering that God is Three-in-One, how does Deuteronomy 6:4 reveal God's "one flesh" design for marriage?

4. From Study Guide 1, explain how Genesis 2:25 is at the apex of the chiasm.

Some people add to the Genesis account concerning relationships between women and men. They take what happened later on in humanity's sinful history and project that back into the Garden of Eden, specifically with the ideas of "hierarchy" and "authority."

Exercise #3: Identify references to human relationships that involve authority in Genesis 1-2.

1. In each of the following passages, God is described as creator and commander. Therefore, God has the authority. From the following passages, who had ultimate authority?
   a. Genesis 2:15

   b. Genesis 2:16

   c. Genesis 2:19

   d. Genesis 2:21-22

2. God also granted authority. To whom did God give authority, and the authority to do what? (Contrast with Genesis 1:16)

	The Man	The Woman
Genesis 1:28		
Genesis 1:29		
Genesis 2:15 with 2:18, 24		

Chapter 4

4. GENESIS 3:1-13, THE ATTACK

One day my professor took all of us who were his doctoral students on a walk over to the magnificent cathedral in Strasbourg, France. There arching over the giant right portal is a series of figures carved in stone standing out from the façade. The figure on the very end is holding out a piece of fruit in her hand.

"This is Eve," our professor said with his thick Alsatian accent. "See! She is holding out an apple and has a smile on her face. She has been standing like this for 700 years."

He motioned to us to step up close and look behind her. We were shocked to see stone snakes imbedded in her shoulders, writhing down her back! The professor commented, "This shows what the sculptor thought of her motivation. He thought she was the Temptress. In front she looks beguiling. But in back she shows signs that she is in league with the serpent!"

This medieval idea is not what the Bible teaches. The Bible says the Tempter in the Garden was the serpent. That is why God cursed the serpent Tempter. And that is one of the reasons why, when we look for a curse on the woman in the Hebrew text, we find none.

Let's think more about that serpent-tempter. He perpetrated the second worst crime in history and also the worst crime in history!

The second worst crime in all history was Satan's murderous attack on the humans in the Garden of Eden. The worst crime in all history was Satan's murderous attack on the sinless second person of the Trinity, Jesus Christ, which resulted in his crucifixion at Calvary.

According to Jesus in John 8:44, Satan has been a murderer since the beginning. He attacked the first woman and man in order to bring about their deaths and he succeeded. Later, he attacked the offspring of the woman, Jesus on the cross.

Did he succeed with that? The Bible says he managed to strike the heel of Jesus, so to speak. But that Jesus would crush his head.

Let's dig deeper. When Satan spoke to Jesus and tempted him at the very beginning of his ministry, Jesus answered Satan. Jesus knew he was speaking to Satan. To do so was not sin. Eve answered Satan too when he spoke to her. When he made an outrageous claim about God's word, she corrected him.

Some people blame the woman for dialoguing with the Devil. Ahh. But that was part of his deceptive attack. The angel Satan had hidden himself using the serpent as a mask.

Had he appeared in the Garden as himself, the most glorious of all the angels, he could have said to her, "*I'm* a godlike creature am I not? My will is the opposite of your creator, your heavenly Father. I say eat the fruit that God has prohibited. Follow my words and not those other words." That would have been honest. That would have been fair.

We learn something right away about Satan. In addition to calling him a murderer from the beginning, Jesus also called him the Father of Lies. Satan began his criminal acts with his masquerade using the serpent. Then he startled the two humans in the Garden with his outrageous suggestion that God had prohibited them from eating of any of the trees in the Garden. His words are found in Genesis 3:1.

Satan was an equal opportunity tempter. He tempted both the woman and the man. The Hebrew text in Genesis 3:1-5 shows him using plural pronouns each time he says "you." In other words, he wasn't aiming his words at just the woman. He was saying you-two, y'all, you-both. And the man was right there listening to all he said.

When the woman defended God's words, Satan made a more frontal attack denying the truth of God's words. In Genesis 3:4 he says, You won't die. Then, in verse 5, he attacks more than God's words. He attacks God and again twists the truth! He makes a counteroffer. Eat this fruit and then you will be like God. He pretends to offer her good knowledge. What he really is offering is for her to know good and evil!

He offered a pack of lies! Having never heard a lie before she turns to her senses for help. Well, the fruit should be good for food. It looks good. Knowledge is good. So she takes the fruit and eats it and offers some to the man who was with her. So what did she do?

What she did stands out in comparison with the man who also ate. Her intent and motives show up in sharp contrast with the man's motives and intent.

Twice in the New Testament we read that she was deceived. Not so for the man. He was different. Perhaps because he wasn't in the middle of Satan's torrent of words as she was, the man was able to look on, so to speak, and evaluate for himself just what was being offered.

Satan camouflaged as an animal was asking the woman to eat something ... good. Satan rebelliously lying about God and setting himself up in the place of God, following his own will, really acted as a model for the man to follow. One modern translation of John 8:44 has Jesus calling Satan the Father of ... Liars." When I read this I began to think of who might have been Satan's first lying offspring. Who would be his first lying child in this way? And then I asked was Satan successful in birthing in the man the seed of a lying heart?

We can get distracted by what happens next. But we should defend against that. The man and the woman end up making fig leaf aprons for themselves. In far back regions of the rainforest I've seen people clothing themselves in simple coverings like that. They make no great fashion statement but it gets the work done. A string of twisted grasses here, tied to a leaf or piece of bark there and voila.

We learn much more of what is in the heart of the first woman and the first man when they speak to God who comes and questions them about what they have done.

After eating, they both knew good and evil. They saw past their nakedness and were ashamed. Their eyes had been opened but not in a desirable way. Their actions showed terrible changes had happened to their one-flesh unity with each other and to their friendship with God.

They used leaves to try to cover themselves from each other! And when God approached, they ran the other way and tried to hide themselves from God! How sad!

When God called, as recorded in Genesis 3:8-12, the man answered as if the woman wasn't there at all. He spoke only of himself: "I heard" - "I was afraid" - "I was naked" - "I hid." It is not like he was used to thinking only of himself. He had not been alone for so very long on the Day they were created. His normal state was together with his wife, as a member of the first family. So why this focus on himself?

Prompting the man by asking pointed questions God asked the man to reveal two facts, "Who told you...?" and "Did you eat...?" The man's evil response revealed many things about him.

There had been three at the Tree. Two of them, the man and Satan-in-the-serpent, were rebels against God's word. But the man didn't tell God about the strange voice that told them to eat. He didn't report what evil lies it had said.

Think about it. God asked, Who told you that you were naked? The answer should have been, Well, actually nobody told me about that. But there was a strange voice at the Tree that told me something. It said you were not good and we could get *further* than you had brought us.

But the man didn't refer to that voice – at all. Instead, the man disobediently did a new evil deed. He blamed both God and the woman as being responsible for the evil he himself had done! He said, "The woman you put here to be with me, she gave me some fruit from the Tree, and I ate it."

God's warning to not eat from that Tree had been deadly serious. The penalty for disobedience was death! The results of death and evil had only begun to show themselves in the man.

God asked the woman, as recorded in Genesis 3:13, "What have you done?" She answered God with no deflection or defiance. She answered God with no accusation. She spoke in a very different way from the man.

> What the Bible tells us about her is not the way she is often presented.

She was deceived no longer. Perhaps as she heard God question the man it all became clear to her. At any rate, now she saw what had happened. In her new wisdom, she recognized evil and said, "The serpent deceived me, and I ate."

In that reply, she unmasked the evil serpent as the source of her deception. And she confessed to the evil she did while deceived – "and I ate."

Had she too committed *more* evil like the man had just done? No. Did she blame the man who was with her? No. Did she accuse God? No. Yet what the Bible tells us about her is not the way she is often presented. And this misrepresentation of her has been going on for a long time.

Degrees of Guilt. What if what happened next took place in a courtroom? Picture God as the judge and the woman and the man as the accused. How should God judge each of them?

People are always judging or misjudging who did what in the Garden of Eden. We can gain insight into what happened there by thinking about the differences between first-degree and second-degree offenders.

The Father of Lies deceived the woman. After she was deceived, the woman took some fruit and took a bite. She gave some to the man who was right there with her and he took a bite. Two bites! These bites were not taken in the same way.

Because the woman ate only after being deceived, she was a second-degree offender. Because the man was not deceived but ate anyway, he was a first-degree offender. He sinned on purpose.

There is a clear distinction drawn between first- and second-degree sinning in the Bible. God makes that distinction in the judgement of the three that comes next in the Garden of Eden. And God does so at other times later in history.

When the people of Israel occupied the Promised Land, God set apart six Cities of Refuge. These were for those who had killed people but were not first-degree, pre-meditated murderers. They were punished. Because life is supremely valuable there were serious consequences for murder. They had to flee their homes to escape the avengers and live in a City of Refuge. But, they were spared swift execution which was reserved for those who had willfully committed first-degree murder. So there was a distinction in how punishment was meted out for those who killed another person. On-purpose, or premeditated first-degree murder received a death sentence. Unplanned or second-degree murder received a lighter sentence. The intent of a person's heart was taken into account by God in Israel and in Eden.

In Eden, each one took a bite. But, their levels of disobedience were different. What was going on in each one's heart was not the same.

Because all of us have been tricked by someone's lies at one point or another what happened at the Tree in the Garden of Eden makes us uncomfortable. When it comes to seeing Satan's outright hostility we shudder and want to turn away. That fits somebody's plan. I'm sure Satan was glad not to be mentioned by the man. And the deceiver Satan doesn't want us to clearly identify him as the source of his ungodly attacks on us in the spiritual realm.

But God sees all of it clearly. And God next judges each of the three at the Tree with perfect justice. God wants us to see clearly too. That's why **it is important to think again about the Bible and get a true picture of what happened in the Garden of Eden.**

[Eve, Strasbourg Cathedral | Coyau / Wikimedia Commons]

Study Guide 4

STUDY: TWO RESPONSES

Our professor had just pointed out a famous sculpture of Eve on the cathedral in Strasbourg, France. He commented, "This shows what the sculptor thought of her motivation. He thought she was the Temptress. In front she looks beguiling. But in back she shows signs that she is in league with the serpent!"

This medieval idea is *not* what the Bible teaches. The Bible says the Tempter in the Garden was the serpent. That is why God cursed the serpent Tempter. And that is one of the reasons why, when we look for a curse on the woman in the Hebrew text, *we find none.*

Exercise #1: Discover the Bible's depiction of the Serpent.

1. The two greatest crimes in human history were perpetrated by the serpent. What were they?

   a. Genesis 3:1-7, 10, 24

   b. Luke 22:3-6, 21-22, 48; 23:44-45

2. From John 8:44, how did Jesus describe Satan?

a. How is Jesus' description supported by the passages in the above passages?

b. How is Jesus' description supported in Genesis 3:1-5?

3. According to Jesus' example in Matthew 4:1-10, is listening to and talking with the serpent a sin?

Satan was an equal opportunity tempter. He tempted both the woman and the man. The Hebrew text in Genesis 3:1-5 shows Satan using plural pronouns each time he says "you." In other words, he wasn't aiming his words at just the woman. He was saying you-two, y'all, you-both. And the man was right there listening to all he said. Neither the woman nor the man had ever heard a lie before.

Exercise #2: Separate the lies and the truth.
1. In reading the apostle Paul's inspired reference in 2 Corinthians 11:3 and 1 Timothy 2:14, who was deceived, and who was not?

2. Who protected and who revealed the true perpetrator in Genesis 3:1-13? Why is this significant?

The woman became a second-degree offender when she ate of the forbidden fruit. She did not sin on purpose. She ate only after being deceived. However, the man became a first-degree offender. He sinned on purpose.

There is a clear distinction drawn between first- and second-degree sinning in the Bible. God makes that distinction in the judgement of the three that comes next in the Garden of Eden. And God does so at other times later in history.

Exercise #3: Discerning the difference between first- and second-degree sin.
1. *Read Joshua 20:1-9, Exodus 21:12-14, Numbers 35:11-12.*
   a. What did God command and why?

    b.   Explain the distinction God made between the crimes and punishments described here.

2.   In Genesis 3:14-17, in what ways did God make a distinction between the man, the woman, and the serpent based upon who or what is cursed? (See passage below.)

Genesis 3:15-17

15 "I will put enmity between you and the woman,
    and between your offspring and <u>her-offspring</u>;
    he will bruise you on the head,
    and you will bruise him on the heel."

16 To the woman he said,
    (Line 1) "I will greatly multiply *your-sorrowful-toil* <u>and-your-conception</u>;
        (Line 2) with-effort you-will-give-birth-to children.
        (Line 3) Your affection is for your husband
        (Line 4) but he will rule over you."

17 And to the man he said,
      "Because you listened the voice of your wife and ate from the tree about which I commanded you, saying, 'You shall not eat of it,' cursed is the ground because of you;
      in *sorrowful-toil* you will eat of it all the days of your life."

People are always judging or misjudging who did what in the Garden of Eden. We can gain insight into what happened there by thinking about the differences between first degree and second-degree offenders.

The Father of Lies deceived the woman. After she was deceived, the woman took some fruit and took a bite. She gave some to the man who was right there with her and he took a bite. Two bites! But, these bites were not taken in the same way.

Because the woman ate only after being deceived, she was a second-degree offender. Because the man was not deceived but ate anyway, he was a first-degree offender. He sinned on purpose. That is why God made a distinction in the judgments on each one.

Chapter 5

5. GENESIS 3:14-15, THE WOMAN'S ENEMY

Joy was just three years old when her family moved across town to another house in south Minneapolis. She went out her front door and came across a neighbor girl playing outside. Her name was Nancy and she was just about Joy's age.

Joy was shy. She planted her feet and clasped her hands behind her back, self-consciously swiveling her upper body to the right and then to the left.

"I like your cowboy hat," Nancy said, trying to make four-year old friendly conversation. "How did *you* know I had a cowboy hat?" Joy asked, surprised that this new friend already knew about her favorite hat!

Then Joy noticed the hat string hanging around her own neck and became aware of the weight of her hat on her back. She had been wearing it all the time! Nancy had noticed. It wasn't hard to see. It was red!

Sometimes others can see something about us better than we can see ourselves. This was certainly true of the man in the Garden of Eden and his

Creator. When the man rebels against God and eats the fruit from the forbidden tree, in his rebellion he follows the one who models rebellion for him. God clearly sees that!

Who is the man following? Certainly not God. Not anymore. God told him not to eat from the Tree of the Knowledge of Good and Evil. But he does just that.

Satan in the serpent addresses *both* the woman and the man at the Tree. We know that because the Hebrew text uses plural pronouns every time Satan says "you." His words are aimed at the man too as recorded in Genesis 3:1-5.

Does Satan come right out and say "Eat that fruit"? Actually, no. But in his twisted way he certainly suggests it.

What about eating fruit from *that* tree too? Both were already practiced eaters of the good fruit in Eden. The woman is deceived into thinking in herself that getting knowledge was good and the fruit of that tree will be good too.

But the man's experience is different. He doesn't focus on the fruit. His focus is elsewhere. In his own mind he believes the tempter's words and focuses on himself.

Here is a short list of things the man does wrong.
1. He doubts God. Satan throws God's words into question. The man does too.
2. He doesn't respect the woman's defense of God's words, as reported in 3:2.
3. He doesn't fear God's wrath. He believes the serpent who lied and said "You will not certainly die" as recorded in 3:4.

Whose voice is the man listening to? It certainly isn't just an animal. The man knows all the animals. He had named them. Not one of them was found to be a fitting partner for him. Why not? He had observed that none of them could relate to him on his level. Yet somehow this talking serpent does!

Another being is talking to him, tempting him to rebel. Does he care who it is? It isn't necessary to know. The temptation is not to focus on another being, but to focus on himself, and on himself apart from his partner and apart from his Creator.

Satan is serving as his model without drawing attention to himself. Satan is rejecting God's word. Satan does not cherish and respect the life in the two humans God has made. Satan lies by masquerading as a serpent, by outrageously mocking God's simple proscription not to eat from one tree, and by baldly contradicting God's word.

In John 8:44 in the HCSB translation Satan is called the Father of Liars. Did Satan succeed in making the man the first in human history of his lying offspring? He plainly did.

When questioned by God the man hides the fact that he has listened to the voice of the serpent. Then the man outrageously accuses God, and the woman, as having caused his actions. So, both the serpent tempter and the man act rebelliously.

God hears the man out then asks the woman what she has done. When she unmasks the deceiver who had hidden himself in the serpent, and then confesses her disobedience to God, God stops the interviews. God does not ask the serpent to speak.

As judge and jury, which the Creator certainly has the right to be, God addresses the serpent, the woman and the man. God's words to the serpent tempter and to the man are strikingly different from God's words to the woman. But we don't usually see *that*.

The Old Testament was written out using the Hebrew language which most of us can't read. So we read what God said using translations into our modern languages. If we are fluent in Hebrew we can notice that the *way* the words and sentences of Genesis 3:14-19 are put together also conveys meaning. God speaks to the serpent tempter and to the man using a parallel six-point pattern. That striking pattern is totally absent in God's words to the woman.

The serpent and the man share many things in common in their rebellion at the Tree. God has noticed. Here are the six points in God's words that are common to both the serpent and the man:

> *These two curses are unlike any other curses in the Bible.*
> *They change the way of things.*
> *Even today, the two curses of Eden are in effect.*

1. God uses the Hebrew word "**curse**" in speaking with each one.

2. The word "**because**" opens each speech as God explains why he is imposing a curse.

3. The **object** God curses is related to each one. "Cursed are *you*," God says to the serpent. And "Cursed is the *ground* ...," God says to the man.

4. Each curse involves **eating** and **dust**. The serpent will "eat dust." The man will eat food that will come from the cursed soil, and eventually, he will return to dust.

5. Each receives a note of lasting **duration**: "... all the days of your life."

6. **Echoing Hebrew verbs** close God's words:

    i.   God tells the serpent: "... bruise (*shuph*) ... bruise (*shuph*)" (The serpent's head will be *bruised* by his enemy.)

    ii. God tells the man: "return (*shuv*) ... return (*shuv*)"

    The man, made out of dust, will *return* to the dust.

God's words to the woman are very different from his words to the serpent and the man because her case is different. She has not purposefully participated in the rebellion at the Tree. God has noticed this too.

She has been deceived, or tricked. God's words to her reflect this. The words addressed to her are different in grammar, logic, tone and content.

The common elements that are found in God's words to the serpent and to the man are missing in God's words to the woman:

- The Hebrew word "**curse**" is not used.

- The word "**because**" is not used.

- The woman is **not cursed**, nor is anything cursed because of her.

- God does not speak to her about **eating** or **dust**.

- The words of **duration**, "all the days of your life," are not used.

- There are **no echoing Hebrew** verbs.

Genesis 3:16 begins with an introductory phrase followed by four lines of words in which God speaks to the woman. Only a total of 11 Hebrew words are used in Lines 1-4. In places, it takes several English words to translate a single Hebrew word.

Genesis 3:16 starts with words of introduction: "God said to-the-woman...." Then:

In **Line 1** of Genesis 3:16, God speaks four Hebrew words:
>#1 Multiplying #2 I-will-multiply
>#3 your-toil
>#4 and-your-conception.

In this Line of the verse, which can be called **Line 1**, God introduces something new. In fact, God does two new things in Line 1. Then, in Lines 2, 3 and 4 God doesn't do anything else that is new. In these lines of the verse God explains and teaches the woman what has happened.

In **Line 2** of Genesis 3:16, God speaks three Hebrew words:
>#5 With-effort #6 you-will-bring-forth #7 children.

In **Line 3** of Genesis 3:16, God speaks two Hebrew words:
>#8 Your-affection [is] #9 for-your-husband

In **Line 4** of Genesis 3:16, God closes with two Hebrew words:
>#10 But-he #11 will-rule-over-you.

It is worth going much deeper into God's words to the woman in Genesis 3:16. But for now, let's go back and focus on God's words to the serpent tempter.

God knows who has been speaking to the two humans at the Tree and how the deceptive masquerade has been accomplished. God deals with both the serpent *animal*, the tool used by Satan, and then God deals directly with *Satan*.

In Genesis 3:14, God takes what the woman has just said and acts on her words.

14 The Lord God said to the serpent,

> "Because you did this,
> Cursed are you more than all cattle
>> and more than all the animals of the field;
> On your belly you will go and dust you will eat
>> all the days of your life."

This is the first of God's two curses in Eden. God curses the body of the serpent. What was its body like before? We can't say. But we do know what serpents are like today. That's because the two curses made in Eden are still in effect today.

The next words God speaks have both an immediate effect in Eden and one forward looking in time. These are recorded in verse 15.

> 15 "I will put enmity between you and the woman
>> And between your seed and her seed;
>> He will bruise you [on the] head
>> And you will bruise him [on the] heel."

God says *I will "put enmity."* What does this mean? Here God confirms these two as combatants. God confirms the woman as the enemy combatant of Satan.

Satan has already attacked her at the tree leading to her disobedience and death. For this, Jesus labeled Satan as "a murderer in the beginning." And the woman has already called him out before God and then repudiated him by her confession before God. If the man has moved to the side of Satan in joining him as a rebel, the woman has moved to God's side in revealing Satan for what he did.

> *If the man has moved to the side of Satan in joining him as a rebel, the woman has moved to God's side in revealing Satan for what he did.*

Then, God spells out the ultimate doom of her enemy which will come through her. Even though he will persist in his attacks and even though figuratively he will bruise the heel of her offspring, who we know ultimately to be Jesus, her offspring will bruise Satan on the head.

In Genesis 3:15, in God's last words to the serpent, God prophesies that the woman's "seed" or "offspring" (*zera‘*) will defeat the Tempter. Bad news for the Tempter, but good news for the woman and all humanity!

When I was starting out in my seminary studies I was told that Genesis 3:15 was a prophecy known as the *protevangelium*. That's a nice long Latin word and it sounded very theological to me. It means the very first mention in the Bible of the good news of salvation.

Somehow I felt right away that this was a strange way to announce the Good News. How could good news be given to the Tempter? It just bothered me. Much later, when my wife Joy pointed out what God says to the woman in the first words in 3:16 is good news, I finally felt good. The full announcement of the Good News starts in 3:15 and spills over into verse 16 when God gives the good news to the woman.

What we should be emphasizing, I believe, are the first words God addresses to the woman along with the last words to the Tempter. The last words in 3:15 are addressed to the Tempter, but are overheard by the woman. She then receives God's promise to multiply her pregnancy, or her conception of the promised offspring.

God tells Satan that the result of his ongoing war with the woman will be his defeat. Then, as God turns to the woman God confirms to her, in Line 1, the good news that she will have ... offspring.

At the start of Line 1 in words 1 and 2 God uses the Hebrew verb "to multiply" twice. It is repeated in two different tenses which can be translated "Multiplying, I will multiply." Then God completes the thought with Hebrew word #4, *heron*, which means "offspring" or "pregnancy." God makes her the promise to greatly multiply her offspring.

Has she eaten the fruit and died? Yes. But there is still to be life after that death. And there will be birth after death. That is the Good News. God gives it to *her*.

The *protevangelium* includes the end of verse 15 and the start of verse 16. But I wasn't taught that in seminary because the second part of that news, the good news, is covered over by the mistranslation of 3:16. **We need a correct translation of Genesis 3:16, a true translation of**

Genesis 3:16 and a better understanding of what really happened in the Garden of Eden.

[Serpent | Pixabay.com]

Study Guide 5

STUDY: FIRST OF TWO CURSES

Sometimes others can see something about us better than we can see ourselves. This was certainly true of the man in the Garden of Eden and his Creator. When the man rebelled against God and ate the fruit from the forbidden tree he followed Satan-in-the-serpent, the one who modeled rebellion for him. God clearly saw that!

Satan addressed *both* the woman and the man at the Tree. We know that because the Hebrew text uses plural pronouns every time Satan said "you." His words were also aimed at the man as recorded in Genesis 3:1-5.

Exercise #1: Determine what the man did wrong.
1. *Read Genesis 2:16-17 and Genesis 3:1-12.*
   a. What did the man learn about the Tree of the Knowledge of Good and Evil from God? From the Serpent?

   b. Who did the man doubt?

2. *Reread Genesis 3:2-6,* remembering the serpent uses the plural form of "you" in its response. Why do you think the man remained silent, and accepted the fruit from Eve?

3. Compare Genesis 2:17 with Genesis 3:4-5, 7, then Genesis 3:8-12, noting a length of time has transpired. What does the man seem no longer to fear?

God's words to the serpent-tempter and to the man are strikingly different from God's words to the woman. God speaks to the serpent-tempter and to the man using a parallel six-point pattern. That striking pattern is totally absent in God's words to the woman.

Speech 1 (vv. 14-15)	Speech 3 (vv. 17-19)
1. "Because *(ki)* you…"	1. "Because *(ki)* you…"
2. "cursed *('arur)* is/are…"	2. "cursed *('arur)* is/are…"
3. object of the curse (serpent)	3. object of the curse (ground)
4. nature of the curse involves "eating"	4. nature of the curse involves "eating"
5. duration of the curse: "all the days of your life"	5. duration of the curse: "all the days of your life"
6. repeated verb: shuph … shuph	6. repeated verb: shuv … shuv

Exercise #2: Note the similarities in language in God's address to the serpent and to the man.

1. What word appears at the beginning of both Genesis 3:14 and 3:17, and what does this signify?

2. After God described the action taken by the serpent in Genesis 3:14, and the man in Genesis 3:17, what did God say would now happen? (The word is identical in both verses)

3. Who is responsible for the action God took in each instance?

4. What two words appear at the end of both Genesis 3:14 and 3:17, and what does this signify?

5. How long will God's action take affect for the man, and the serpent?

6. What verb is echoed in Genesis 3:15? How is this pattern repeated in Genesis 3:19?

The serpent and the man shared many things in common in their rebellion at the Tree. However, the woman's case was different. Having been deceived, she had not purposefully participated in this rebellion, and God's word reflected this.

Exercise #3: Identify the differences between God's words to the woman, and God's words to the serpent and the man.
(Refer back to the points in Exercise #2)
1. *Read Genesis 3:12-14.* Upon whose testimony does God base His response?

2. *Read Genesis 3:14-19* and compare the six points in God's speeches to the man and serpent, with God's speech to the woman. What six elements found in God's word to the serpent and man are missing in God's speech to the woman?
   a. _____
   b. _____
   c. _____
   d. _____
   e. _____
   f. _____

After God's cursing of the body of the serpent, comes Genesis 3:15, a prophecy known as the *protevangelium*, the good news of salvation. In Genesis 3:15, in God's last words to the serpent, God prophesies that the woman's "seed" or "offspring" (*zera'*) will defeat the Tempter. Bad news for the Tempter, but good news for the woman and all humanity!

God tells Satan that the result of his ongoing war with the woman will be his defeat. Then, as God turns to the woman God confirms to her, in Line 1, the good news that she will have . . . offspring. Has she eaten the fruit and died? Yes. But there is still to be life after that death. And there will be birth after death. That is the Good News. God gives it to *her*.

Exercise #4: In the passage below, identify the bad news for Satan and the good news for the woman.

Genesis 3:15-17

15 "I will put enmity between you and the woman,
    and between your offspring and **her-offspring**;
    he will bruise you on the head,
    and you will bruise him on the heel."

16 To the woman he said,
    (Line 1) "I will greatly multiply ***your-sorrowful-toil* and-your-conception**;
    (Line 2) with effort you will give birth to children.
    (Line 3) Your affection is for your husband
    (Line 4) but he will rule over you."

17 And to the man he said,
    "Because you listened the voice of your wife and ate from the tree about which I commanded you, saying, 'You shall not eat of it,' cursed is the ground because of you;
    in ***sorrowful-toil*** you will eat of it all the days of your life."

Chapter 6

6. GENESIS 3:15-17, THE HIDDEN PATTERNS

 In the days before GPS technology, a propeller-driven, six-seater single-engine missionary plane took off from a grass airstrip heading out across the raw African rainforest. The destination? Another isolated grass strip more than a hundred miles away.

A while after taking off into a clear blue sky, before it could get there, the ground below was covered by a thick layer of clouds that went on and on and on. Time passed. Where was the airstrip? An attempted landing any place other than that hand prepared airstrip would result in a terrible crash.

The pilot asked the passengers to pray, then help look for a gap in the clouds so he could get oriented. Eventually they would have to descend into those clouds to set down.

Finally one of them spotted a gap in the clouds. The pilot looked, recognized a land mark and based on that insight immediately banked the plane down into a rapid descent. As the plane descended below the cloud layer the way to the airstrip was clear.

I've been in planes like that. And, I've felt like the six in that little plane who found that gap in the clouds.

The meaning of some verses in the Bible has been clouded as well. For me the greatest insight through confusing clouds came when my wife, Dr. Joy Fleming, told me **she had found the keys** to unlocking the reading in Hebrew of God's words to the woman in the Garden of Eden in Genesis 3:16.

Using those key insights to navigate she opens up the meaning of God's words to the woman given to her after God addresses the serpent tempter in 3:14-15. Many people think God cursed the woman in some way and even perversely reordered relations between men and women in Genesis 3:16.

Some people reject a God who would say things like they think was said in this verse. Others, grit their teeth and hang on as they read through the words in their English translations waiting till they get out of the clouded mess that seems to cover the verses at the end of Genesis chapter 3.

When that pilot took off from the grass airstrip part of the success of the pilot in finding a landing place came in knowing the lay of the land. Also, the pilot knew the landmarks and could navigate by them.

In her doctoral research my wife discovered a clear *pattern* written into Genesis 2-3. These two chapters are put together using a seven-part pattern that is a chiasm.

A chiasm! A chiasm can be pictured like a rainbow or as a bell curve. In a chiasm the theme or words used in a first line or section (let's call it A) are repeated in the corresponding section at the end (A' or A prime). Likewise with the second section from the beginning (B) and the next to the last section (B'). A chiastic pattern works this way until the center section is arrived at. That section is often the key or turning point to the chiasm.

In Genesis chapter 2 God creates the man and puts him in the Garden of Eden. Then, God continues to create and relate until the summit is reached in 2:25. In chapter 3, Satan attacks and there is a sharp downward slope. The corresponding beginning and end sections of A and A' in

Genesis 2 and 3 are that in A God places the man in the Garden of Eden and in A' God drives the man out from the Garden.

The discovery of the precise *parts* of the Genesis 2-3 passage provides the overview or the map of the terrain in Eden, so to speak. As Joy became convinced that these chapters were written in this pattern **she discovered the sub-patterns** that tie ideas together in the Hebrew text. She noticed that God's words to the serpent tempter and the man both contained the same key Hebrew words following a parallel pattern but that God's words addressed in between to the woman did not use that vocabulary or follow that pattern at all.

She noted however that God's words to the woman did connect in a particular way to God's words to the other two characters, addressed after and before her. This occurs in God's first four Hebrew words spoken to the woman in Line 1 of Genesis 3:16. The four Hebrew words take several more words to translate into English: Multiplying I-will-multiply your-sorrowful-toil and-your-conception.

Then one day while reading a journal article by Dr. Isaac Kikawada about a smaller word pattern way over in Genesis chapter 11, she had a gap-in-the-clouds moment. As Kikawada analyzed the structure of that passage he referred to a similar structure located in Genesis chapter 2.

A linchpin! Did Kikawada refer to Genesis 2? That drew her attention. That's *my* passage, she thought. If there was a recognizable special word pattern in Genesis chapter 2 in the first section of the upward curve of the passage, then we might expect to find a similar word pattern in the corresponding slope on the downhill side in Genesis chapter 3. Here's the linchpin pattern in Genesis chapter 2:

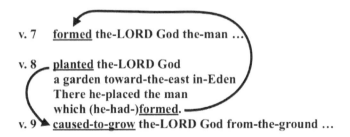

v. 7 formed the-LORD God the-man ...

v. 8 planted the-LORD God
a garden toward-the-east in-Eden
There he-placed the man
which (he-had-)formed.

v. 9 caused-to-grow the-LORD God from-the-ground ...

That's what she had been noticing for some time in her research. A significant word pattern, a linchpin pattern, centered in the four words of *Line 1* of Genesis 3:16 linked the words in this verse to the words in the verse after and the one before it. But she had never come across anyone commenting on that. And even here, Kikawada was only commenting on Genesis 2.

People who earn a master's degree are supposed to gain a mastery of what is known about something. People who become a doctor with a research degree are supposed to go beyond the master's level. They are supposed to reveal something new, something to add to our knowledge in their field of study. Had she found something new here? More importantly, were there revelations from God in the text of the Bible that had been overlooked, or that had somehow been obscured over the years?

As we peer through the clouds that have been covering over Genesis 3 and look there for two landmark linking words, a linchpin construction becomes clear.

In Genesis 11 and Genesis 2, key words in the center section of linchpin constructions are linked to the same or similar words below and above their center sections. As pointed out by Kikawada, in the Genesis 2 linchpin, in verse 8 in the middle, God brings together both plant life and *humanity*. Kikawada shows that this important "linking" takes place not only in *what* the words say but also in the *way* the words are arranged. The initial Hebrew word "planted" of verse 8 points down to verse 9 to the *similar* Hebrew word "made-grow." The *last* Hebrew word in verse 8, "formed," points back to the Hebrew word "formed" in verse 7.

When she read the remarks by Kikawada on Genesis chapter 2, my wife banked her plane, so to speak, and dove down for a closer look at the details of what she had found to verify that the patterns in Section A and Section A' of Genesis 2 and 3 corresponded. Sure enough. Like Genesis 2:7-9, Genesis 3:15-17 is put together with a middle section having two key

> *Genesis 3:16 is formed as a linchpin construction with two key words linked to 3:17 and 3:15!*

words linking it to the verses around it. So, the first Hebrew words of

Genesis 3:16 form the center of a linchpin construction with two key words linked to 3:17 and 3:15!

As it turns out, recognizing *this* is very important when it comes to understanding these words and translating them into our modern languages. Missing the presence of this linchpin construction contributes to the *mis*translation and *mis*understanding of this very important verse. So it is necessary to think again and to nail down what is going on here in Hebrew.

As in the first linchpin, in Genesis 2, there are two words in 3:16 that link to the verses around it. The Hebrew word "sorrowful-toil" in verse 16 links down to the same Hebrew word, "sorrowful-toil," in the verse after it. The Hebrew word, "conception," in verse 16 links back to the similar Hebrew word "seed" or "offspring" in the verse before it. This precise way of arranging these words did not happen by accident. It is one of the ways Hebrew is written out to deliver information in a memorable way.

The first linking Hebrew word in 3:16 is 'itsabon. It means "sorrowful-toil" and points down to the same Hebrew word used in verse 17. There God tells the man that the curse on the ground made because of him will result for him in 'itsabon or "sorrowful-toil." In fieldwork each one, the woman and the man, would have 'itsabon or "sorrowful-toil."

And they weren't to be the only ones. All humanity regardless of gender is subject to this 'itsabon, this "sorrowful-toil," for we all have to deal in some way with the ground that God cursed because of the man.

> *All humanity regardless of gender is subject to 'itsabon,*
> *"sorrowful-toil," for we all have to deal in some way with the*
> *ground that God cursed because of the man.*

The word 'itsabon is used only three times in the Old Testament. The third and last time it is used is instructive. In Genesis 5:29 a new child is born. He is named Noah. We've all heard of him. The name Noah means "relief," "rest" or "comfort," which means relief from 'itsabon, relief from sorrowful toil! Here is what the verse says where it uses the word 'itsabon: "Now he called his name Noah, saying, "This one will give us rest from our work and from the sorrowful toil of our hands caused by the ground which the Lord has cursed."

This "sorrowful toil of our hands" is true for the parents of Noah as well as for the first two humans in the Garden of Eden. It is not something that only applies to the woman in Eden, and it is not something to do with the act of childbirth as many modern versions would have us believe. It has to do with the sorrowful toil of our hands as we work the cursed ground.

The *second* linking Hebrew word is used at the end of Line 1 of 3:16. It is *heron* which means "pregnancy" or "conception" and it points back to verse 15 to the Hebrew word *zera'* which means "seed" or "offspring."

A literal translation of the four Hebrew words of Line 1 of Genesis 3:16 in English would be as follows: (1) Multiplying (2) I-will-multiply (3) your-sorrowful-toil (4) and-your-conception. There is nothing in these words about the process of giving birth. *These* words are tied into the difficulty of fieldwork as in 3:17 *and* into the promise of the woman's conception of multiplied offspring who would vanquish Satan.

But, have you noticed in the English translation of the Bible you typically refer to that you can't make out the linking words of Line 1? Almost all modern translations don't correctly translate the last two of these four words. They write out Line 1 of 3:16 as if it is talking about pain-in-childbirth! They incorrectly treat the Hebrew words of the linchpin as if they can be merged into just one idea, and a new and different idea at that. They could do this if they had grammatical justification to do this. They could do it if in these words there were an indication of the presence of what's called a hendiadys. But there are no such grammatical indications and the structure of the linchpin forbids doing so.

Modern English versions have been confusing readers by attempting to squeeze into one idea the important two different and contrasting linking words and ideas in Line 1 of Genesis 3:16! They invent a single new idea that totally breaks the links that should be followed to the verses after and before it.

This is equivalent to covering over God's inspired Hebrew with the repugnant word pollution of ideas God's didn't put there. And the different ideas contained in this word pollution have flowed downstream causing confusion and contradiction. This has created major damage in the translation and interpretation of a half dozen key passages in the New Testament.

Here is the wrong idea that gets plastered thickly over God's words in Line 1 of 3:16. It is the wrong-headed idea that God in some way basically curses the woman at the very end of her 9-month-long pregnancy.

Here are just three translations that word Line 1 of 3:16 this way.

HCSB: I will intensify your labor pains
NIV: I will greatly increase your pains in childbearing
NASB: I will greatly multiply your pain in childbirth

Can they do this?
They are doing this!
But *should* they do this?

Let me take you back to an interesting meeting we had when we were thinking about whether or not a hendiadys might be located in Line 1 of 3:16.

One crisp autumn, Joy's studies led us to New England. This area of the country is especially beautiful when the leaves change color. It is also the home of several renowned research schools and libraries. So she scheduled a visit with an Old Testament professor at a famous school and asked me to accompany her.

As we went down the half flight of stairs to his office entry, a few copper colored leaves swirled around our ankles in the autumn breeze. Inside, his office was crammed with books.

We found space to sit and talk about the "and" in Line 1 of Genesis 3:16. "Professor, would you look at this Hebrew 'and' and tell us what you see?"

His comments, punctuated by long pauses as he reflected deeply, ran something like this:

Here we have an example of a hendiadys – two things joined by 'and' to mean a different thing.

... Yes, an example of a hendiadys. ... Of course, **this one doesn't look like your ordinary hendiadys.** *The typical indicators are not present. ...*

In fact, there is nothing in the grammar to indicate that the words in this verse should be combined as if there were a hendiadys present.

The words 'itsabon and heron could very well be read normally as two separate things with 'and' in between joining them. ...

But, even though **this doesn't look anything like a hendiadys** *and it could be correct to say there is no hendiadys here ... we know that it is a hendiadys.*

"Thank you so very much, professor," Joy said when the time came to a close. As we climbed up the stairs into the breeze and the leaves that greeted us, one thing was perfectly clear to us from our hour-long discussion on the word "and." **There *wasn't any reason* to drop it out.**

There wasn't any reason to push the words together in Line 1 even though the professor had said, "We *know* it is a hendiadys." Perhaps he was influenced by the writings of others who had passed along the incorrect assumption that this was a hendiadys. But, the professor's observations, made in front of us, clearly showed that the widely held view wasn't necessarily correct.

Without squeezing the words of Line 1 into a hendiadys, the math in Genesis 3:16, Line 1, is easy to calculate: *One* thing, plus *one more* thing, joined by the word "and" adds up to *two* different things—"sorrowful-toil *and* conception." Line 1 does *not* add up to one *new* thing—"pain-in-childbearing"!

To illustrate how the Hebrew grammar in Line 1 works, let's look at the *distributive property* in this diagram:

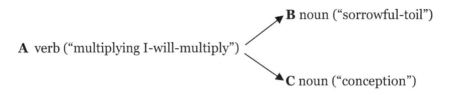

B noun ("sorrowful-toil")

A verb ("multiplying I-will-multiply")

C noun ("conception")

The resulting meaning is that God will surely multiply "sorrowful-toil" *and also* that God will surely multiply the woman's "conception." God is going to multiply, not one, but two things. That's what a good translation should show us. But that's not what's out there in practically every translation. Here's the linchpin in Genesis 3:

> 3:15 I will put enmity ... between your seed and her <u>seed</u>
> He shall bruise you on the head
> And you shall bruise him on the heel.
> 3:16 I will greatly multiply your <u>toil</u> and your <u>conception</u>
>
> 3:17 Cursed is the ground ... in <u>toil</u> you shall eat of it ...

Joy's discovery uncovers *a major error* that modern translations are making in the way they are wording Genesis 3:16 into English. And the more we look at it the more it becomes clear that this is a BIG PROBLEM!

Have *you* ever wondered why God appears to be so harsh with the woman in 3:16? So have others. They have asked, "If she was treated this way by God then did she somehow deserve it? And if she deserved what was practically a curse imposed only on her just think of how bad she must have been."

To treat her this way goes along the lines of the man's accusation that she had been his temptress. That was a false charge. The man had also blamed God. Both ideas were wildly incorrect! Neither the woman nor God tempted the man. Satan-in-the-serpent tempted the man.

Why would the man blame her, treating her as if she were his enemy? She was the enemy of the serpent. God had confirmed her as Satan's adversary.

Might this powerful adversary be working behind the scenes to twist the translation of God's actual words to the woman in Genesis 3:16? It would be a master stroke against her in public opinion. It would lead to serious mistreatment of women by those who thought her deserving of severe punishment.

God, on the other hand, treated the woman with respect. God warned her that she would have sorrowful-toil in participating in field work just as would the man, her fellow farmer, when they worked the fields God had cursed because of the man.

God then built on his creation blessing to her. God promised that she would have multiplied pregnancy. And one of her offspring would be the Messiah.

In his defiant challenge to God, the man dared to accuse God of being his tempter. And then the man had also blamed the woman as being his tempter. Neither charge was correct. And modern translations that promote the idea that God changed the last hours of her conception and pregnancy into a special moment of punishment are incorrect as well.

We need to let Genesis 3:16 communicate its message to us clearly without the word pollution. And **we need to spread the true meaning of 3:16.**

Study Guide 6

STUDY: UNCOVERED PATTERNS

As with a missionary plane, searching for a gap in the cloud cover, the meaning of some verses in the Bible has been clouded over as well. For me the greatest insight through confusing clouds came when my wife, Dr. Joy Fleming, told me she had found the key to unlocking the reading in Hebrew of God's words to the woman in the Garden of Eden in Genesis 3:16.

In her doctoral research my wife discovered a clear pattern written into Genesis 2-3—a seven-part pattern that is a chiasm. A chiasm can be pictured as a rainbow or as a bell curve.

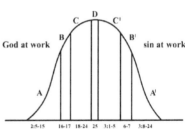

Exercise #1: Describe the chiasm.

1. *Read Genesis 2:25.* (Review from Chapter and Study Guide 1)

    Genesis 2-3 is formed as a chiasm. Genesis 2:5-24 is the upward curve of God at work, and Genesis 3:1-24 is the downward curve of sin at work. Genesis 2:25 is at the summit. Compare the two sides of this chiasm. What do you see?

    a.   Genesis 2:5-15 with Genesis 3:8-24 (A and A')

    b.   Genesis 2:16-17 with Genesis 3:6-7 (B and B')

    c.   Genesis 2:18-24 with Genesis 3:1-5 (C and C')

    d.   How does Genesis 2:25 act as the summit? (D)

2.   *Read Genesis 2:7-9 with Genesis 3:15-17 (diagrams below).*

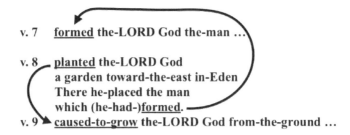

    a.   How does the word "planted" in 2:8 connect with verse 9 below it?

    b.   How does the word "formed" in 2:8 connect with verse 7 above it?

3.   From the text below, how does the word "sorrowful-toil" in Genesis 3:16 act in the same way (as outlined in question 2 above) with 3:17? How does the word "conception" in 3:16 act in the same way with 3:15?

> **3:15 I will put enmity ... between your seed and her <u>seed</u>**
> **He shall bruise you on the head**
> **And you shall bruise him on the heel.**
> **3:16 I will greatly multiply your <u>toil</u> and your <u>conception</u>**
>
> **3:17 Cursed is the ground ... in <u>toil</u> you shall eat of it ...**

    This precise way of arranging these words did not happen by accident. It is one of the ways Hebrew is written out to deliver information in a memorable way.

    In Line 1 of 3:16 the *first* linking Hebrew word *'itsabon* which means "sorrowful-toil" points down to the same word used in verse 17. There God tells the man that the curse on the ground made because of him will result in *'itsabon* or "sorrowful-toil." In fieldwork each one, the woman and the man, would have *'itsabon* or "sorrowful-toil."

In Line 1 of 3:16, the *second* linking Hebrew word *heron* which means "pregnancy" or "conception" points back to verse 15 and the Hebrew word *zera'* which means "seed" or "offspring".

A literal translation of the four Hebrew words of Line 1 of Genesis 3:16 in English would be as follows: (1) Multiplying (2) I-will-multiply (3) your-sorrowful-toil (4) *and*-your-conception.

Often, in trying to discern how to think about a Biblical character's actions and words, we look to God's response to help us.

Exercise #2: Discern God's response.

1. From Genesis 3:11-12 which two beings did the man say had led him astray?

2. From Genesis 3:13 who did the woman say had deceived her?

3. What two words found in Genesis 3:14 and 3:17 (missing in God's response in Genesis 3:16) reveal who *God* found culpable?

4. *Read Genesis 3:14-19*, with the correct translation of Genesis 3:15-17 above. List positives and negatives you see in God's message to
   a. The Serpent:

   b. The Woman:

   c. The Man:

   What do these lists reveal about God's response to each?

5. How might Genesis 3:12, 3:15 and 3:16 shed light on why Genesis 3:16 is so often mistranslated and misinterpreted?

Chapter 7

7. GENESIS 3:16, THE 11 TRUE WORDS

What comes to your mind when I say the words "natural childbirth?" In the months before we left our studies in France beside the Rhine River to head for the rainforests of the Congo, we learned that we were pregnant with our first child! Friends counseled us that it might be difficult to have to deliver our first little one on an isolated missionary station somewhere in the Ubangi.

So we set out to prepare ourselves as best we could. A few blocks from our student apartment we bought several books in French about natural childbirth. Nothing available in English, but we were in France after all and this was in the days before the Internet.

Joy and I worked hard to understand the specialized vocabulary. The emphasis seemed to be concentrated on breathing exercises. That was no surprise This was the country of Dr. Lamaze (pictured above).

Joy was 6 months pregnant when we finally arrived in hot steamy Africa.

Right away we noticed the happiness in everyone's faces when they saw we were pregnant – well, that Joy was pregnant. In Europe and America having babies brings about a positive response from family and friends, but less so from strangers. This was surely not true where we lived in Africa. Having babies was considered to be wonderful!

We looked forward to the birth of our child as well. We didn't know if we were having a boy or a girl. We had tried to find out at the public hospital in France but results were inconclusive.

Finally, Joy gave birth to our first child in a mission hospital in the rain forests of northwestern Congo. Around sunset on a Sunday evening, after 36 hours of exhausting contractions, Joy was invited to ride in the cab of the doctor's pickup truck and he drove them over to the hospital. A flock of red-tailed gray African parrots flew overhead. Palm trees stood sentinel duty and a ten-foot high termite hive was tinted pink by the setting sun. There was no ultramodern delivery room available. The setting was more like a field hospital during World War II.

On the short trip the doctor stopped at the small powerhouse to start the diesel-powered generator. At least we would have lights on and a rotating overhead fan during the delivery in that stifling room.

The medical staff was superb. The lead doctor was ably assisted by two other doctors. Both of them were Harvard Medical School graduates. Plus, there were several fine nurses in attendance.

A nurse and I stood on either side of Joy as we timed her breathing. She received no medication of any kind. I admired her great effort, which was followed by exhaustion and exhilaration, as Joy gave birth to our wonderful baby girl, Christy!

Was it a cursed experience I asked Joy as we looked back on it the next morning? No. It wasn't. But it certainly required a lot of effort.

Conception, and pregnancy, was intended to be a good and natural process when God created woman. Even after Satan's attack, their disobedience and the beginning of living life in their now *mortal* bodies, the promise of future conception and pregnancy was a good and natural event. It remains a good and natural event.

God does not change the woman's body as he speaks to her in Eden. Yet modern translations make it appear that God somehow zaps the woman, changing childbirth into a bad thing.

To understand Genesis 3:16 we must recognize that in God's first words to the woman in Line 1 of Genesis 3:16, God didn't even touch on the subject of childbirth. (1) God spoke to her about shared sorrowful-toil (*'itsabon*) in field work and (2) God spoke to her about conception or pregnancy (*heron*) and especially of the offspring who would bruise Satan's head.

The *way* the words are put together in the chiasm of Genesis chapters 2 and 3 carries meaning. And the *way* verses 15-17 are linked together in a linchpin construction by the two key words in Line 1 of Genesis 3:16 brings meaning. But the meaning of *each word* itself is also important.

In the two words of the linchpin construction that link God's words to her with God's words to the man and to the serpent the woman learns two things. Neither of them is a curse on her. One thing is about bad news. One thing is about good news.

The bad news she learns is that when God curses the ground because of the man it will affect her too. They both will experience *'itsabon* or "sorrowful toil" as they do field work to raise food from the cursed ground outside of Eden. God knows they will be going there and what life there will be like. So God describes to her what her experience will be like with the cursed ground. She will have *'itsabon.* She will have sorrowful-toil. That is bad news.

But God immediately moves on to tell her of good news. How can the words of 3:16 be taken as good news right after God's stern judgment on the serpent tempter? Simple math. Three of the four words in Line 1 ring of good news! Here are the four Hebrew words of Line 1: *harbah 'arbeh 'itsabonek wheronek,* multiplying, I will multiply, your sorrowful toil, (and) your conception.

Genesis 3:16, Line 1. "God acts." The first two words in Line 1 of 3:16 (*harbah 'arbeh*) are the repetition of a single Hebrew verb "to multiply" or "multiplying, I will multiply." This same verb in this same verbal construction which is repeated for emphasis will be used in association with God's blessing on the "seed" or "offspring" (*zera'*) of Abraham later in Genesis.

When God blesses Abraham for being willing to sacrifice his son Isaac, God first repeats the word "to bless" for emphasis. Then God repeats the word "to multiply" for emphasis, as in Genesis 3:16. God also uses this verb and verbal construction of "multiplying, I will multiply your descendants" (*harbah 'arbeh zera'*) when he speaks to Hagar in Genesis 16.

God says to Abraham in Genesis 22:17, "...*blessing* I will *bless* you, and *multiplying* I will *multiply* your descendants (*zera'*) as the stars of the heaven and as the sand which *is* on the seashore...."

Suppose, there had been someone who was familiar with God's blessing on Abraham who had somehow never come across the chapters on the Garden of Eden. When they came to God's repetition of the verb "to multiply" in Genesis 3:16 they would have expected the word "seed" or "offspring" (*zera'*) to come next.

In Genesis 3:16, we might expect God to say to the woman that he will greatly multiply her descendants (*zera'*) —*harbah 'arbeh zera'*, as God says to Abraham and to Hagar. We find this, but in the form of a linchpin. The word *zera'* is used just a few words earlier—in verse 15, as the words point back to the first mention of the Gospel. In 3:16, a similar word that fits the sound pattern better in 3:16 – *heron* – is used. In words 1, 2 and 4 of Line 1 God says, "multiplying, I-will-multiply" "your-*heron.*" *Heron* means "your-conception" or "your-pregnancy." *Harbah 'arbeh ...* your-*heron.*

It is wonderful to hear from God that she will assuredly have offspring. God had blessed her and the man on Day 6 of Creation. "Be fruitful and *multiply*" God had said. And it is wonderful to hear from God that assuredly she will have offspring so that she can fulfill the promise that her offspring will defeat her attacker, Satan.

It is almost startling to recognize what God clearly says to the woman. We have become so used to thinking of her deserving special punishment as if she was the Temptress – which she was not, that it is hard for us to focus on what God actually says. God gently warns her, in advance, of the coming curse on the ground and then God completes the announcement of the *protevangelium* of the Good News and glorious Gospel that she will yet bear offspring who will defeat Satan.

When God introduces her to the sorrowful toil or *'itsabon* she will experience outside of Eden, God is not telling her about something reserved for her and not the man. The man will experience this exact same sorrowful toil or *'itsabon* because it is something God will do to the ground because of him! They both will have sorrowful-toil because of the curse on the ground God will make because of the man.

Noah's father used this same word in Genesis 5:29. There *'itsabon* is described as something both he and his wife are experiencing. All these years after the Garden of Eden people are thinking of this specific sorrowful toil that is bothering them because of the curse on the soil. It is the sorrowful toil of **our** hands in working the cursed ground, he says.

Genesis 3:16, Lines 2-4. "God instructs." With these mostly positive first four Hebrew words in mind, *can* we concentrate on what God says next? Try to keep in mind the two actions God promised to take in Line 1 and then get ready for the next three lines God says to her in Hebrew. The two things God tells her about in Line 1 are (1) sorrowful-toil in fieldwork and (2) conception.

In Lines 2, 3 and 4 God tells the woman about how things have turned out as the result of Satan's attack on them and their disobedience. In these three Lines God *instructs* the woman. God looks at the various areas of her life and tells her things she needs to know.

God's words to the woman in verse 16, Lines 2-4 are words of instruction. They are words of description and of teaching. In them, God tells the woman what her physical experience will now be like.

God also knows that she is married to a dead man. Her husband was a willful participant in the Great Disobedience. Clear signs are showing how badly his relationships with God and his wife have been corrupted.

Very soon they will find themselves outside of Eden with the way back barred by armed angel warriors. With supreme urgency and maximum use of every word, God instructs the woman in Lines 2, 3 and 4.

Two things will have changed which will have a physical impact on the woman, her mortality and the curse on the ground. (1) There is now *death*, and she has a mortal body – this consequence of sin was foretold in

Genesis 2:17. (2) There will be the *curse on the ground*. She will experience "sorrowful toil," which will be the result of a separate act of God (Genesis 3:17).

Having disobeyed God's prohibition, her body is now subject to difficulty and death. But God does not curse her body, as God just did the serpent. The changes she will experience come from these other two causes rather than a curse, or a "zap" from God. The changes will come about (1) because she is now mortal and (2) because the ground will be cursed.

In **Line 2 of Genesis 3:16**, the first thing God explains is the actual process of childbirth. It is important to notice, *Line 1* of 3:16 does not refer to *pain* in childbirth. It doesn't refer to childbirth at all. But, *Line 2* does speak about the event of childbirth.

Translations have gotten so caught up in their inventions that they make God seem to stutter, saying once in Line 2 and somehow back in Line 1 something about childbirth. But that is not what God says. God acts in Line 1 in two ways (that we've noted). In Lines 2-4 God describes and teaches the woman what the entrance of sin and death will mean.

> God *acts* in Line 1 of Genesis 3:16
> God *describes and teaches* in Lines 2, 3 and 4

The first Hebrew word in Line 2 is *b"etsev*. It means "with effort" or "with work." This word is used elsewhere in the Old Testament. Elsewhere *'etsev* never describes anything to do with childbirth, although it does here.

Let me illustrate. Deep winter in Minnesota where we live now brings snowdrifts in one's driveway, or even across the road. It is not too unusual for someone to get stuck in a snowdrift several feet high. When that happens, it's sometimes necessary to get help getting pushed out.

Those who do the pushing have to strive mightily to help the driver get enough traction and momentum to move the car out of the drift. The work can be painful as it takes great effort to push the car out.

This is what is meant by Hebrew word #5 in Genesis 3:16 – "**with-effort**." In *this* way, "with effort," the woman will bring children into the world.

God is telling the woman that now that she has a mortal body she should not think that she is dying when she feels the contractions of labor. When she pushes out her precious offspring it will require the use of muscles that will involve effort.

Only after conception and nine months of pregnancy (Hebrew word #4 of Line 1) comes childbirth. In the environment outside of Eden (where God knows she and the man will soon find themselves), childbirth will be different for the woman. She will give birth with a mortal body subject to difficulty and even death.

Here's a summary of what we find in the Hebrew text of Genesis 3:16:

First, God tells the woman of *two* certain actions.
One *links down* to the curse on the ground because of the man
(verse 16 *'itsabon* ⟶ verse 17 *'itsabon*).
One *links back* to the promise of the birth of Offspring who will crush
the tempter
(verse 15 *zera'* ⟵ verse 16 *heron*).

Genesis 3:16 (Line 1) **I will surely multiply (1) your sorrowful toil in fieldwork *and* (2) your conception.**

Then, God instructs the woman about what has happened,
to her and to them, now that they are mortal and fallen.

(Line 2) **With effort you will bring forth children**
(Line 3) **Your [loving] desire [is] to your husband**
(Line 4) **But he [is rebelliously ruling over himself and] will rule over you.**

We had one more childbirth in our little family unit. Seven years after Christy's birth, we had just returned from Africa and were in Minnesota when it came time for Mark to be born. This time Joy asked in advance if she might have an anesthetic, only if and when she needed it. The staff assured her that would be just fine.

She waited until that moment did arrive, and asked for an anesthetic. "Oh, it's too late to ask for that now," she was told. "You should have asked *earlier* in the process. Taking anything this close to the delivery is not possible now."

And so, once in a jungle hospital, and once in a western hospital, she experienced very "natural" childbirth. She gave birth through her own intense *effort* (and with God's help).

What about Line 2 of Genesis 3:16? In line 2, when God explains this sort of childbirth to the first mother-to-be in Line 2, God describes it to her in such a way that she will understand what is happening without the benefit of having watched any other human mother give birth before. Line 2, in Genesis 3:16, is extraordinarily sensitive, clinical and respectful. *"Effort"* – hard physical work requiring endurance – is going to be her experience in childbirth. She will bring life into the world with *'etsev.*

This description of how the first woman will experience *birth* with her mortal body, contrasts greatly with what God tells the man when God addresses him. God tells him about *death.* His mortal body will die. It will return to the dust from which God made it. In both cases, God teaches the first couple what to expect, giving them insight into the implications of their mortality as mortal human beings.

The rest of Line 2 rushes to an additional piece of information that God reveals to the woman. She can still fulfill God's creation mandate from Day Six recorded in Genesis 1 to "be fruitful and multiply." She will bear *more* than one child. The plural word is used. She will have children!

Thus far God has used a collective singular word in Line 1 of 3:16 and in 3:15 that can mean "just one" or possibly "a number of." The "offspring" (*zera'*) and the "pregnancy" (*heron*) referred to in 3:15 and Line 1 of 3:16 might have meant she would have just one child. But at the end of Line 2 in 3:16 God uses the word *banim.* It is the plural word for "children." After her first born child she will bear more. She'll have at least two children for sure. And likely more as God's blessing is worked out and she bears children who will fill the earth!

What about Line 3 of Genesis 3:16? In Line 3, God looks into her heart. God instructs her on the state of her heart and contrasts it with the state of her husband's heart. How much has changed for her in the paradise she lives in? Patiently, lovingly God instructs her on the state of her heart.

Her affection is still for her husband. This is implied in just two Hebrew words. One is: "Your-desire" (*teshuqah*). And the other word is: "to-your-husband."

No verb is used here. When this happens in Hebrew, the verb "to be" or "is" is typically inserted in English. Her-desire "is."

What kind of "desire" is this? There is every reason to assume this is a healthy desire, as she had before the attack. And God says her desire "is" still the same.

Some have attempted to compare her "desire" in 3:16 to another desire depicted in the word picture in Genesis 4:7. But the verse in 4:7 is outside of the tightly constructed chiasm of which 3:16 is a part. It is outside of the passage of 2:4-3:24.

The "desire" mentioned in Genesis 4 is only part of the next passage. What we learn from that occurrence is that the word "desire" (*teshuqah*) is not necessarily a term reserved for human affection because it is used in a non-sexual way in the account of Cain and Abel.

The word *teshuqah* is used only one other time in the Old Testament. It is helpful to our understanding because it describes another human. In Song of Solomon 7:10, *teshuqah* is used to describe Solomon. His lover refers to Solomon's "desire" in these words – "I am my beloved's and his *desire* is toward me." There is no negative connotation to his desire for his lover.

The word "desire" is *not* used for the man when God refers to him in Line 4 of Genesis 3:16. God's evaluation of the woman's heart will serve as a measuring point when the state of the man's heart is compared to the loving *desire* of his wife.

It is not so easy for modern readers to simply recognize her desire as her affection. This is because many, many, people for 700 years and more have identified her as a shameless Temptress, a ravening beast who led the man to his death and deserved a curse. If that were truly the case, then in Line 3 of 3:16 we could expect God to talk about how terrible her heart has become.

Theologians have actually taught this. H. C. Leupold said the woman had a morbid yearning. He and others have even said that she was a nymphomaniac!

Notice the confusion that the following translations reveal when it comes to Line 3 in 3:16. Many translations assume her desire was somehow bad. They can't agree on what way her desire was bad but they freely invent interpretations of the meaning of desire.

Here is a representative sampling of translations of Line 3 in Genesis 3:16:

> "Your desire shall be *contrary* to your husband...."
>
> *English Standard Version*
>
> "you will desire to *control* your husband...."
>
> *New Living Translation*
>
> "since your *trust* is turning toward your husband...."
>
> *International Standard Version*
>
> *"You will want to control your husband...."*
>
> *NET Bible*
>
> "Yet, you *will long* for your husband...."
>
> *God's WORD Translation*
>
> "and thy *submission shall be* to thy husband...."
>
> Brenton Septuagint Translation
>
> "and thou *shalt be* under thy husband's power...."
>
> *Douay Rheims Bible*

Where did all these ideas come from! Remember, the two Hebrew words in Line 3 say simply: your-desire (is) to-your-husband. And the meaning is simple and straightforward. She has not turned against her husband. She still desires him.

What about Line 4 of 3:16? In Line 4 God describes the state of the man's heart. The Hebrew words in Lines 3 and 4 practically vibrate with tension as the man's heart is contrasted with the woman's heart. The man's heart is very different.

God tells the woman, "He will rule (the verb is *mashal*) over you." Unlike Line 3 where God described the woman using a noun and the preposition "to" or "toward," here we encounter adversarial words. In Line

4 a preposition and a verb (not a noun) are used to describe the man. The verb is *mashal* or "rule." The preposition is "over."

In Line 3 the preposition used for the woman is 'to' or 'toward'—suggesting a relationship of equal partners. In Line 4 an aggressive adversarial verb is used along with the preposition "over." The words "rule" and "over" stand in marked contrast to the affection of the noun and preposition attributed to the woman in the preceding line.

This verb for "rule" in Line 4 is not the same Hebrew verb that was used in Genesis 1, even though it looks the same for English readers because translations use the same English word for the two different Hebrew verbs.

When God commanded the man and the woman to *rule* over the rest of creation in Genesis 1:28, the verb *radah* was used. This was a legitimate ruling, sometimes called the Creation Mandate. The humans were to be in charge of all creation.

When the man's prospective action in 3:16 is described, however, the verb *mashal* is used. This is the same verb that is used to describe the ugly *ruling over* perpetrated by the Philistines in Judges 14:4.

Line 4 describes a relationship that is not the equal partnership God instituted in Genesis 2. This is one person "lording it over" the other. God describes this as what will go on. He does not say it is his will for it to happen. These words are descriptive, not prescriptive.

God does not give a command to the man to go and rule over the woman in Line 4 of 3:16. God is not even speaking to the man in 3:16!

In Lines 2-4 God has been telling the woman about life after the attack. With effort she will bring forth children. Her desire is to her husband. On that she has not changed. BUT the man has changed. "But, he will rule over you" (!).

The man has aligned himself with the murderous liar who spoke to them through the serpent. He has hidden the tempter's part in their eating the fruit of the Tree. He has accused God and blamed her of being the cause of his rebellion. And now God warns her that she is married to the most sinful man in the world. That sinner rejected God's rule and started ruling over himself, going his own way. And he was going to continue to reject God's rule over him and over her. The man was going to usurp God's place in ruling over her and he was going to rule over her himself!

Have you known the Bible says these things in 3:16? It does. But most people aren't getting its message because of the mistranslations and misinterpretations of it. That's why I founded the Tru316 Project and Tru316.com and I'm praying for people to be raised up to correct our translations of 3:16 and more!

God's word is a pure source of life to people worldwide. But we need to remove the word pollution that is harming those who come to the Bible expecting to be refreshed and instead are repulsed by the pollution they find. **We need the *true* message of Genesis 3:16.**

(The hospital where our first child was born)

[Dr. Fernand Lamaze | Lamaze International (http://www.lamaze.org)]

Study Guide 7

STUDY: THE 11 HEBREW WORDS

It was no surprise that the French books Joy and I read to prepare for our first experience in childbirth emphasized breathing exercises. This was France, the country of Dr. Lamaze.

Joy was 6 months pregnant when we arrived in hot steamy Africa. Then, she finally gave birth to our first child in a mission hospital in the rain forests of northwestern Congo. Around sunset on a Sunday evening, after 36 hours of exhausting contractions and hard work, Joy was driven across the mission station grounds to the hospital.

A nurse and I were on either side of Joy as we timed her breathing. She received no medication of any kind. I admired her great effort, which was followed by exhilaration, as Joy gave birth to our wonderful baby girl, Christy!

"Was it a cursed experience?" I asked Joy as we looked back on it the next morning? "No. It wasn't. But it certainly required a lot of effort."

Exercise #1: Identify the bad news and the good news God gave to the woman.

1. *Read Genesis 3:14-19*, with the correct translation of Genesis 3:15-17 below.

a. What bad news did the woman hear?

- Genesis 3:15

- Genesis 3:16 (along with 3:17)

b. What good news did the woman hear (*harbah 'arbeh*)?

- Compare Genesis 22:17 "with that blessing I bless you, and multiplying I multiply your seed as stars of the heavens, and as sand which is on the sea-shore" with Genesis 3:16. What do you notice?

- Genesis 3:15

- Genesis 3:16 (compare with Genesis 1:28)

2. How will having a mortal body, experiencing *'etsev*, now affect the woman?

a. Genesis 3:16 (compare with Proverbs 5:10, 14:23,)

b. Genesis 3:19

3. How does Genesis 3:16 describe change in the man, and how would this affect the woman? (See Line 4.)

Genesis 3:16

16 To the woman he said,
    (Line 1) "I will greatly multiply **your-sorrowful-toil** <u>**and-your-conception**</u>;
    (Line 2) with effort you will give birth to children.
    (Line 3) Your desire is for your husband
    (Line 4) but he will rule over you."

Exercise #2: Analyze the heart motivations in both the woman and the man.

God addressed matters of the woman's heart in a particular way, revealing both the woman's heart with regard to the man, and the man's heart with regard to her.

1 . a. How might Genesis 2:23-25 inform how the word "desire" is to be understood in this context? (Compare also with Song of Solomon 7:10)

   b.   Why is Genesis 4:7 not a good comparison verse?

2. a. Compare Genesis 2:23-25 with Genesis 3:16. What has changed in the man's heart?

   b.   In what way does comparing Genesis 2:20 with Genesis 3:20 further reveal this change?

   c.   How had the man corrupted the meaning of God's words to them in Genesis 1:28?

Chapter 8

8. GENESIS 3:17-20, GOD JUDGES ADAM

In Genesis chapter 2 we learn that God created Adam and then placed him *in* the Garden of Eden. At the end of Genesis chapter 3 we read the shocking news that because of what Adam did there God drove him *out* of the Garden of Eden and placed an angelic guard to keep him from reentering it! How should we feel about Adam?

Wouldn't you love to live in the Garden of Eden? I would! Of course none of us now lives in the Garden of Eden, so we know he never made it back in. But he was there – for a while.

What should we think of him, and how he lived and loved in the Garden?

The Attack. Historically, theologians have talked of the man's *fall* in the Garden of Eden. Chapter headings are added to Bibles in which chapter 3 is labeled as "The Fall." I have been preferring a different heading for some time now. If we add any heading at all, I think it shouldn't be "Chapter 3 - The Fall" but "Genesis Chapter 3 - The Attack."

The man and woman didn't just fall in the Garden like some over ripe fruit that reaches a point where it separates from its stem and plops, or falls to the ground. That is inevitable. The man's fall was not.

Life ahead in the Garden was properly planned for a long and well-lived fellowship with the woman and with God. When God created the human couple on Day Six of Creation God evaluated the situation. It was very good. That included the man.

But something catastrophic happened. It was the *hateful* attack by Satan on the woman and the man at the Tree of the Knowledge of Good and Evil.

I learned something about the intensity of that *hate* from a painting by Michelangelo at the base of the wall of the Sistine Chapel at the Vatican in Rome. I was a senior in college on spring break. Through a series of remarkable events I was on a 9-day tour of Israel with stops on the way out and back in Paris and Rome. (Pictured above.)

Ah Rome! Everyone on a whirlwind tour of the capital city of Italy has to visit the masterworks of Michelangelo on the ceiling and on the front wall of the famous Sistine Chapel. So I was there along with a moving herd of visitors craning our necks and gawking at a succession of paintings far too numerous to fully take in. There was a signal given of some kind and everyone began to move back and head out to see another remarkable sight.

But I stayed behind. I lingered. I wanted to let at least something soak in. Something I could capture and keep in mind in the years ahead.

I happened to be standing close to the front wall that is covered with the huge painting of The Last Judgement. On one side of God the Father angels are helping the souls of the saved up into the regions of eternal bliss and reward. On the other side demons are driving the souls of the damned down into the netherworld for everlasting and awful punishment.

In front of the wall is a free standing altar with the figure of Christ dying on the cross. It is covered in gold.

And then I saw *it*. On the wall itself near the bottom to the left, glaring up from an opening out of hell looking like the mouth of a cave was a demon. It was triumphant in an exaggerated and ugly way. It was ecstatic. Nothing that evil should ever be that enthusiastic. But it was. Why, I asked staggering back to look at it better.

And then I realized why. It was staring out at Christ up on that cross. It was gleeful that Jesus, the lamb of God, had been pinned to that tree and was suffering and dying, or perhaps was already dead. And it thought, We have won and I am *glad*!

An attendant finally noticed me, that last tourist in the room, and he shuttled me out to make room for the next herd of tourists to come in for their turn. And so that experience was over. But I never forgot that wall. And Jesus on that lonely cross. And that gleeful demon.

Clearly, he was painted to represent the thinking of Satan. I have killed again. I have killed my chief enemy!

How awful! How ugly!

In John 8:44 the Devil is described as "a murderer from the beginning." And so he murdered Adam and Eve in the beginning. Jesus called him the Father of Lies. Here is the full text of verse 44. Jesus is speaking to his hateful critics: "You are of your father the devil, and you want to do the *desires* of your father. He was a murderer from the beginning, and does not stand in the truth because there is no truth in him. Whenever he speaks a lie, he speaks from his own nature, for he is a liar and the father of lies."

This is who attacked the woman and the man in the Garden. Whether we gain artistic insight or hear the very words of truth from the mouth of Jesus it is important to keep in mind just who attacked them in the beginning.

The man's model. And so in the Garden the man listens to the words of the serpent tempter. And he makes the intent and actions of Satan *his own*. He too rebels against God.

Step by step he moves away from God and toward Satan!

- Has Satan just thrown God's words into question in 3:1? Apparently the man does too.
- Does the man look with respect on the woman's defense of God's words reported in 3:2? We don't read that he joins her in correcting the word of the serpent tempter.

- Does he respect God's warning against eating resulting in punishment? He apparently believes the serpent enough who lies and says "You will *not* surely die" according to 3:4.
- Doesn't he already know about good? God had named the Tree the Tree of the Knowledge of Good and Evil. Does he want extra knowledge, to know evil?

And so, he eats the forbidden fruit.

> *The man takes the intent and actions of Satan*
> *and makes them* his own *as he too rebels against God!*

When God judges the three at the Tree, God groups the man together with Satan in his words of judgment. God treats *the woman* apart from these two rebels because she doesn't rebel on purpose. She disobeys only after being deceived.

God makes six points in addressing the serpent. And then God uses those same six points and much of the same exact wording, even to the repetition of sounds when he addresses the man. The way this passage is written out in Hebrew adds to the meaning of the words that are used.

This repeated pattern of six common elements ties the two of them together in God's evaluation of their intent and acts.

God warns the woman in Genesis 3:16 that the man has changed. Starting with the way he responded to the serpent's words, then when he hid from God, and finally when he accused God and her, the man was now very different from the man she had married on Day Six. And God knew this. God told her that her heart hadn't changed - she still desired him - but that the man would rule over her, taking God's proper place in ruling over her - just as the man had rejected God's proper place in ruling over him.

So how does the man set about ruling over her? Before she was created it became very clear that there was no other being on earth like the man. He was alone, by himself. And that was "not good."

At the end of Day Six, God would bless the man and the woman together and command them to subdue the earth and to rule over all the earth. This is described in Genesis 1:28. God blesses the woman and man and commands them both to rule (the Hebrew word is *radah*) over the animals and the rest of the created realm that God made for them. The man exercises a legitimate ruling when he names the animals just before the woman was created. Then God makes the woman and there are two humans, equal partners.

When the man names the animals in Genesis 2 he uses what is called *the naming formula*. It is found elsewhere in the Bible. It sounds something similar to a king or a queen who knights someone. "I dub you, Sir Lancelot." And in this way the new knight receives a title from the ruler who is the overlord. The naming formula in Hebrew includes the specific verb, *qarah* ("to call"), followed by the noun, *shem* ("name"). In the Hebrew record of Genesis 2 the naming formula is used to describe when the man *called the names* for each animal over whom he ruled. And thus he named them.

When God creates the woman, recounted in Genesis chapter 2, the man does not name her. Not at all. What he blurts out so enthusiastically is his recognition that finally here is his partner.

She is not another furry friend. As recorded in Genesis 2:23 the man says, "This is now bone of my bones and flesh of my flesh."

He doesn't name her but tells how she is like him. He recognizes her as 'woman' for she was taken out of 'man.' He is *'ish*, the male human and she is *'ishshah*, the female human.

Adam and Eve? Not yet. In Genesis 5:2, in Hebrew, we learn that God named this pair *adam*. The Hebrew naming formula is used here in 5:2 as God ruled over them both.

God gave this one name to both the woman and the man at creation. The name *adam* means "humankind" or "human being." In keeping with God's name for both of them, we could refer to them as "Mr. and Mrs. Adam."

But out of the blue a separate name for her is coming! At the end of God's words in Genesis 3:16, God alerts the woman to changes in her partner. God explains to her that the man is about to engage in a very different way of relating to her other than in equal partnership. God tells the woman, "But he will rule (*mashal*) over you." Where did this idea come from? Was it a good ruling over?

This was not the ruling over that God gave to them both on Day Six of Creation, as recorded in Genesis chapter 1. The Hebrew verb there was *radah*. The *mashal* kind of ruling, that God describes in Genesis 3:16, was a far different and inappropriate kind of ruling. This was the kind of ruling exercised by the evil Philistines as described in Judges 14:4 who exercised a cruel oppression over Israel!

God had not told either human to rule over the other. The one who did this would be disobeying, breaking God's order from what had been put in place on Day Six of Creation. For one human to rule over the other human, one human would first have to choose self-rule, rejecting God's rule over him and the order God had made. The man was going to usurp God's place in ruling over the woman and he was going to rule over her himself! The one ruled over by the other human would be faced with a terrible reality: "We each owe obedience to God who rules over us, so how do I deal with this human who is trying to rule over me in God's place?"

> The man was going to usurp God's place in ruling over the woman and he was going to rule over her himself!

As soon as God stops speaking words of judgement to the man, in Genesis 3:20 the man's first act is to *call* her a new *name*. The wording is clear. Sadly, the Hebrew naming formula *is* used here. The man dubs the woman like he dubbed the animals. We could translate verse 20 as follows: "Now the man *called* the *name* of his wife Eve because she became the mother of all alive."

The man (shall we now refer to him as Adam?) stunningly treats her like the animals who were beneath him. Here is the sinful start of what many label as patriarchy. And the Bible traces the path of this sinful practice down through history.

This is not something instituted by God. Certainly not! This is the hateful act of the rebellious man as he participated in the Great Rebellion against God that took place in the Garden!

Knowing what he had already done, and that he was inclined to mistreat his partner, God pronounces his words of judgment on the man in verses 17-19 of Genesis chapter three.

Judgement? Here is Genesis 3:17, "And to the man he said, Because you heeded the voice of your wife and ate from the tree concerning which I had commanded you saying, You shall not eat of it...." The issue raised here by God is, Did you follow my voice or another voice? Voices?? The man had *followed* the voice of the serpent tempter, had *blamed* the voice of the woman, and had *disobeyed* God's voice.

Based on this, God imposes judgement in verses 17-19, starting with a curse because of the man's willful sin.

> Verse 17: Cursed is the ground because of you. In sorrowful toil you will eat of it all the days of your life. Verse 18: thorns and thistles it will sprout for you and you will eat the herbs of the field. Verse 19: By the sweat of your face you will eat bread until you return to the ground from which you were taken. For dust you are and to dust you will return.

"Cursed is the ground because of you." When God addresses the man, God's first act of business is to identify the man's sin and the state of the man's heart when he sinned. The sentence of death for sin had already been announced and had occurred. It was non-negotiable. Spiritual death had already occurred. Physical death was already at work in his now mortal body.

Who, or what, is cursed? The man heard God address the serpent. He heard God say to the serpent, "Because *you* have done this, cursed are *you*...." When God began speaking to the man, the man may have anticipated receiving a similar punishment, "Because *you* man have done this, cursed are *you*...."

But, God does not curse the man. Instead, God *deflects* the curse. It hits the ground (*'adamah*, in Hebrew) from which the man (*'adam*) was made, "Cursed is the *ground* because of you...." Whew! That was close.

The grace of God is a marvel! Neither human is cursed – neither the woman who sinned after being deceived – nor the man who sinned willfully in the first degree.

The loving Creator treats them justly but graciously. They both die, but neither one is cursed.

After the curse on the soil is imposed *because of the man*, God, as his divine teacher, explains to the man how death and the curse will affect him. The man learns (1) that he will experience "sorrowful toil" because of this curse on the soil. He also learns (2) that indeed his days are numbered. He will die and return to the dust.

Had the man desired to be like God? God teaches the man that as a result of the curse on the ground he will experience something new but completely undesirable: "in 'sorrowful toil' you will eat of it all the days of your life...." The curse on the ground will make raising food much harder. The man will have to toil over it. This toil will raise sweat on his brow, and every time this happens, in sorrow he will remember why the ground has been cursed.

The woman has already heard from God, in verse 16, that she will experience this same "sorrowful toil." For her, the announcement was a proleptic prophecy. The result was foretold but the cause for the result was not immediately given.

Now the woman overhears where this "sorrowful toil" will come from, and why it will come about. It comes about through God's curse on the soil because of the rebellion of the man. She will experience this sorrowful toil as she walks the same earth and works the same cursed soil with her hands as will the man.

Many, too many, modern translations make it appear that when God tells the woman about impending "sorrowful toil" (*'itsebon)* in Genesis 3:16, God tells her about something unique to her. They make it look like something is imposed on the woman because of what she did. However, *'itsebon* in verse 16 is the same "sorrowful toil" spoken of in verse 17 that is the result of the curse God places on the ground because of the man!

The "sorrowful toil" has nothing to do with her being a woman, or with her bearing children. It has everything to do with working the cursed soil, which she and the man will do when they are outside the Garden.

The man and the woman had been undisputed rulers over all the animals and plants. Now, the cursed soil will produce unwanted thorns and thistles. The man will experience difficulty and diminished returns as he works the cursed ground. As one of the designated rulers over the soil, he will have a rebellious subject.

As God details for the woman a correct yet gentle description of how she would expend "effort" in bearing children in verse 16, in verse 19 God gives the man a very different message. He gets details on dying! No awful words here about being eaten by worms in the grave. God correctly but gently tells the man what will happen: He will return to the dust from which he came.

God's words in the Garden are packed with meaning. The serpent tempter, the woman and the man all overhear what God says to the others. All are informed by this open process.

The man overhears God speak to the serpent tempter about the coming Offspring of the woman who would crush his head. The man overhears God's words of concern to the woman, alerting her that the man's heart is no longer full of a loving attitude for her and that he will rule both over himself apart from God and over her.

The man hears that the soil will be cursed because of *him*! He learns of the "sorrowful toil" that will result. The man hears that his life will end and that his body that was drawn from the dust will return to the dust. Then, God's words of judgment and description come to an end.

Throughout the ages, God's strength, purity, love and justice largely have been forgotten. Apart from the true God, humans create gods and spirits that are corrupt. They are pictured as having all the flaws that sinful humans see in themselves, because fallen humans cannot imagine anything higher than themselves.

In much the same way, people who look back in time from outside of Eden, have difficulty imagining a truly good picture of sinless spouses relating to each other.

This is one reason **the first chapters of Genesis are so important.** They go beyond our fallen imaginations and introduce us to how it was, and what God designed us to be! It tells us how we are meant to be, as individuals in our relationship with God, and if married, in our relationship with our spouse.

[Sistine Chapel, Last Judgment | Michelangelo, Public domain, via Wikimedia.com]

Study Guide 8

STUDY: JUDGMENT ON ADAM

Don't think "Genesis chapter 3 - The Fall" but rather "Genesis chapter 3 - The Attack."

The man and woman didn't just *fall* in the Garden like some over ripe fruit that reaches a point where it separates from its stem and plops, or falls to the ground. That is inevitable. The man's fall was not.

Life ahead in the Garden of Eden was properly planned for a long and well-lived life in fellowship with the woman and with God. When God created the human couple on Day Six of Creation God evaluated the situation. It was very good. That included the man.

But something catastrophic happened. It was the *hateful* attack by Satan on the woman and the man at the Tree of the Knowledge of Good and Evil. I learned something about the level of that hate from a painting by Michelangelo at the base of the wall of the Sistine Chapel at the Vatican in Rome—Satan's minion was gleeful at the crucifixion of the Lamb of God. Described as a murderer from the beginning (John 8:44), the Devil was delighted at the downfall of these two human beings.

Exercise #1: Describe what life held in store before Satan's attack.

1.   *Read Genesis 1-2.*

    a.   Name each area of creation that is good.

    b.   Describe what God blesses. What does it mean to be blessed? (Use a Bible dictionary for help)

2.   a. From Genesis 1:26-27, how would human beings be an image of God on earth?

    b.   According to Genesis 1:28-30, in what ways did God bless human beings?

3.   What authority did God assign to each domain, and what authority did God retain?

4.   What further blessings are described in Genesis 2?

5.   Compare Genesis 2:7 with 15-16, Genesis 2:19-20, and Genesis 2:18 with 2:22-25. Describe the man's relationship with God, with the earth, with creatures, with woman, and within himself (see Genesis 2:25).

When God judged the three at the Tree, God grouped the man together with Satan in his words of judgment. God treated *the woman* apart from these two rebels because she did not rebel on purpose. She disobeyed only after being deceived.

God made six points in addressing the serpent. And then God used those same six points and exact wording, even to the repetition of sounds when he addressed the man. The way this passage is written out in Hebrew adds to the meaning of the words that are used. This repeated pattern of six common elements tied the two of them together in God's evaluation of their intent and acts.

Exercise #2: Identify the change in the man.

1. *Read Genesis 2-3.*

   By comparing each of the following passages, identify how each of the man's relationships has changed because of what he had done.

   a. With God: Genesis 2:7-9 with Genesis 3:12, and 22-24.

   b. With the earth: Genesis 2:8, 15 with Genesis 3: 17-19.

   c. With creatures: Genesis 2:19-20 with Genesis 3:21.

   d. With the woman: Genesis 2:19-20 with Genesis 3:12, 16, and 20.

   e. Within himself: Genesis 2:25 with Genesis 3:7.

2. Consider the shift of value in the name the man gives to the woman in light of Genesis 3:15, and the name the man retains for himself: Adam means "human being." What do you think the man wanted to retain power over?

3. Compare the verb *radah*, found in Genesis 1:28, with the verb *mashal,* found in Judges 14:4. In what way would the man now rule, particularly with regard to the woman?

A FINAL WORD

. . . AND NEXT STEPS

The Book of Eden simply would not have been possible without the doctoral research of Dr. Joy Fleming, my wife. I highly recommend reading the summary of her dissertation in *Man and Woman in Biblical Unity, Theology from Genesis 2-3*. Both her complete doctoral dissertation, as well as her summary (in ebook and audiobook), are available from the website of the Tru316 Project: www.Tru316.com

Acknowledgments

To our parents who helped us find Jesus as Savior and lovingly sacrificed for us.

To our children and their spouses, Christy and Jeff and Mark and Bobbie, who have been very supportive.

To the believers of our home churches who encouraged us all along the way - Hope Church in Akron, Ohio and First Free Church in Minneapolis, Minnesota.

To our professors and mentors at Wheaton College and Trinity International University who challenged and equipped us – Walter C. Kaiser, Jr, Kenneth S. Kantzer, Alan Johnson, Herb Wolf, Ruth Bamford, Zondra Lindblade, J. Herbert Kane, John R. W. Stott, Paul E. Little, Arnold T. Olson, Walter L. Liefeld and others.

To our friends in Strasbourg, France – Daniel and Josiane Bresch, François and Sylvie Martin and Eric and Marie Thé Dietrich

To our EFCA Mission colleagues – Lester Westlund, Robert Dillon, Beverly Nyberg, David and Karen Oldberg and many others.

To our Bangui Evangelical Graduate School of Theology / Faculté de Théologie Évangélique de Bangui (BEST/FATEB) family members – Ade Mokoko, Thomas Touangaï, Isaac Zokoué, René Daïdonso, Nupanga Weanzana and many more.

To our work and school colleagues – Dick Lundborg, Nancy Moyer Graves, John M. Newton, Jr., Judy Austin, Brian and MaryAnn Nystrom and many more.

And, to Judy Douglass, Daryl F. Busby, Leslie Leyland Fields, Alice Mathews and Walter Kaiser for their endorsements of our work.

Students and Team Members of the Tru316 Project Workshops

Joanna and Joanne provided technical assistance and Gary, Donald, Ann, Janet and many more encouraged me, asked good questions, and gave valuable feedback that helped shape the final form of the Workshop lectures that take a deep dive into the key passages most affected by the mistranslation of Genesis 3:16. The original presentations can be purchased at Tru316.com/shop, and are also available on YouTube. This series is called the "Think Again Tru316 Workshops" that cover:

1. The 7 Key Passages on Women and Men Corrected (Overview)
2. Genesis 3:16—Eve, Part 1 (No Curse on the Woman)
3. Genesis 3:16—Eve, Part 2 (Eve vs. the Tempter)
4. Genesis 3:17-20—Adam, Disobedience in the First Degree
5. Genesis 3:14-15, 17-19—Adam & the Tempter (the 2 Rebels)
6. Genesis 3:16: Deep Dive
7. 1 Peter 3:1-6—The Weaker Husband (unbeliever)
8. 1 Peter 3:7—The Weaker Wife (unbeliever)

https://www.youtube.com/c/Tru316ProjectGenesis316andbeyond

Correcting Genesis 3:16 freed me to think again about the key New Testament passages. I did my doctoral research on two of these passages, Ephesians 5-6 and 1 Timothy 2-3. I invite you to get and read my simple three-chapter book, *Women and Men in the Light of Eden*. In it I summarize what we've just covered on Genesis and I spell out with clarity what I discovered in Ephesians and 1 Timothy. This book, *Women and Men in the Light of Eden*, is written in non-technical language and can be easily understood by anyone who studies the Bible.

Here are the three chapters in *Women and Men in the Light of Eden*. Each chapter has study questions at the end.

Chapter 1: Genesis 2-3, Together with God in the Garden.

Chapter 2: Ephesians 5-6, Together with Christ in the Church.

Chapter 3: 1 Timothy 2-3, Corrected and Restored by Christ.

Take action!

Here's a shout out to the pioneers who have already joined, and to the builders who are joining now in taking action to clean up the pollution that has streamed from the mistranslations of Genesis 3:16.

You can become a part of this growing movement to correct Bible mistranslations and teachings that promote error in God's words to the woman in Genesis 3:16 and beyond. By reading this book and taking courses such as **The Eden Course** found on the website, Tru316.com, you first equip yourself. The next move is to teach others the correct translation and true reading of Genesis 3:16.

Finally, thanks to the Tru316 Patreon pioneers: Donald B. Johnson, Leaona and Mike E. F. Huston, Joanna Plum, Ann Jones, Janet Roth, Gene Bourland, Nahla Petro, Joanne Guarnieri Hagemeyer, Jan M. Carnes, Loes Tam, Les LaMotte and Ron Hesselgrave. Here's the link to join them: www.Patreon.com/Tru316Project.

Genesis 3:16 is a wonderful verse and so are the passages throughout the Bible that are related to it. But they need to be clearly translated and clearly taught. Most of all, we need a tru316.

15162797R00070